A Sailor's Guide to Wind, Waves and Tides

Captain Alex Simpson, BSc.

WATERLINE

Copyright © 1996 by Alex Simpson

First published in the UK in 1996

British Library Cataloguing in Publication Data
A catalogue record for this book
is available from the British Library

ISBN 1 85310 571 6

Typeset by Servis Filmsetting Ltd, Manchester
Printed in England by Livesey Ltd, Shrewsbury

Waterline Books
an imprint of Airlife Publishing Ltd
101 Longden Road, Shrewsbury SY3 9EB

Contents

Introduction

There can be few situations in which one is more continually aware of wind and weather than at sea. The smaller the craft, the more intimate that awareness. In this book an attempt is made to describe in reasonably simple terms the origin and development of weather systems and their effect at sea, the nature of waves and tides and the behaviour of ships and boats in sea conditions.

The earth carries its atmosphere and its waters in daily rotation and at the same time orbits the sun from which it receives heat. The result is a general global circulation of prevailing winds and ocean currents. Within this circulation weather systems are formed and developed with varying properties of mainly cloud, rain and wind. The seas respond with wave motion varying from calm to storm. The moon attracts the waters of the earth causing the periodic rise and fall and circulation of the tides.

The following chapters deal with the causes of weather at different latitudes and the effects as experienced at sea. The theory of tides and of progressive and standing waves is applied to description of tidal movement in oceans and the rise and fall and ebb and flow in coastal waters. Some elements of the stability of vessels are included and applied to their behaviour in ocean waves and in shallow or narrow waters, concluding with some suggestions on action which might be taken in the conditions described.

CHAPTER 1

Wind and Weather

The mariner's first interest in any weather forecast is surely the force and direction of the wind. Under sail attention to wind is obvious. Masters of ships throughout all the years of sail must have spent much of their waking hours in contemplation of the wind and its possible changes and no doubt had it in mind in their sleep as well. But all ships and boats, no matter what their size or means of propulsion, have to take account of wind because wind causes wave motion. The state of the sea affects all that floats and all on board. Wind is movement of air. There are vertical winds and upper winds and the horizontal surface winds which generate wavelets, slight waves, moderate waves and storm waves.

Air is held round the earth by gravity and since it is compressible it is most dense at the earth's surface becoming rarefied with height. Indeed, most of it is compressed within a few kilometres of the surface in a layer known as the troposphere. It is within the troposphere that the ever-changing movement and conditions of temperature and moisture-content cause our weather. The upper boundary of the troposphere is the tropopause, which is about ten kilometres high at the poles and about fifteen kilometres high at the equator. Well before these upper limits are reached the air has so reduced in density that it cannot support human life, hence the pressurised interiors of aircraft. Above the tropopause is the stratosphere, the upper part of which contains the well known ozone layer which reflects the sun's ultra-violet radiation. Above the stratosphere there are discontinuities of temperature gradient which identify layers or spheres. Within these and more important to the mariner are the layers of ionised gases, the ionosphere, which reflect radio waves back to earth and allow long distance radio communication.

Air is mostly nitrogen with a little more than twenty per cent life-supporting oxygen and a very little carbon dioxide and other elements. Most important from the weather point of view is its water vapour content. Water vapour is always present in the air in varying quantities and is responsible for cloud, rain, hail, snow, dew, frost, mist and fog. For the present however, we shall give our attention to the movement of air.

The earth is rotating rapidly west to east carrying its air with it. At the same time its surface is subject to daily and seasonal heating by the sun. This gives rise to a general circulation of air causing winds which prevail in direction over the earth's surface, especially over the oceans. Energy is radiated from the sun in all directions into space and the earth receives the small proportion which happens to arrive at its position as it travels in orbit around the sun. This comes as short wave radiation a little of which, in the ultra-violet range, is absorbed forming the layers of the ionosphere and below that the ozone layer, but mainly passes through the atmosphere with little weather effect. On striking the earth's surface, land or sea, it produces heat.

On land much of the heat does not get beyond the surface layers. In the ocean the radiation is absorbed to a greater depth and the heat is more widely dispersed. The heated surfaces then re-radiate back into space. At very much lower temperature than the emission from the sun, the radiation is of a longer wavelength with the property of heating the air through which it passes. Air is thus heated from the ground upwards. Generally therefore, air is warmest at ground level and its temperature falls with altitude.

At night with the sun gone the earth loses its heat. It is the water vapour in the air which absorbs the earth's radiation. When cloud is formed much of the heat is trapped and prevented from escaping out into space. On a clear night with no cloud, much of the day's heat will be lost while on a cloudy night the heat is retained and there is less drop in temperature.

The fall in temperature with height within the troposphere depends much upon the source of the air. If it comes from a warm area it might be cooled at ground level and get warmer above the ground. In any circumstances at the upper boundary, the tropopause, it will have fallen to below minus fifty degrees Celsius. Above that there is some rise in temperature through the stratosphere then a fall and rise again through the layers know as

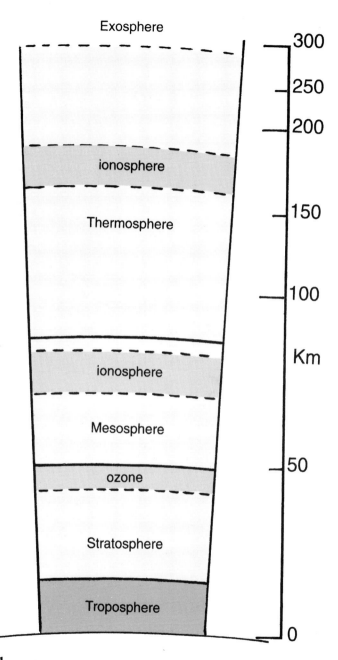

Fig 1

the mesosphere and the thermosphere. These have little weather significance but it is within these heights that the ionosphere is formed.

The air is held round the earth by gravity and its weight exerts a pressure on the earth's surface. This is atmospheric pressure which is measured by the barometer. Air like other gases expands when heated. It is then less dense than colder air. Cooler denser air thus causes higher atmospheric pressure than warmer less dense air. Also pressure decreases with height. As we go higher there is less air above and therefore less weight. Within the troposphere the rate at which pressure decreases with height is virtually constant.

Warmer air in cooler surroundings will tend to rise and allow the cooler air to flow in on the surface to take its place. As the air rises it encounters less pressure and expands. Expansion causes a lowering of temperature. The temperature falls at a rate equal to that of reduction of pressure which is constant. Dry rising air actually cools at one degree Celsius every hundred metres or ten degrees Celsius per kilometre. This is cooling due to rising which is known as adiabatic cooling and the rate of cooling of rising air is known as the adiabatic lapse rate. Still air neither rising nor falling, normally suffers fall in temperature with height. That fall in temperature is variable and may even be reversed. It depends upon the environment and is known as the environmental lapse rate.

Thus rising air cools at a fixed rate and is surrounded by air which cools with height at a rate which may be greater or less than the fixed rate. Obviously the rising air will go on rising as long as its surroundings are colder and will stop rising only when its temperature is equal to its surroundings. At the same time colder air is flowing in along the ground. At the height where the air has stopped rising it will take a direction of flow in response to the circulation set up below.

The descending cold air is similarly heated due to falling and the overall result is clearly one of a circulation of air from high pressure to low pressure at the ground, rising at the low pressure area and flowing as an upper wind towards the high pressure area then descending to continue the circulation.

In the tropics the sun passes overhead or nearly overhead on its daily path from rising to setting. In polar regions it is much lower

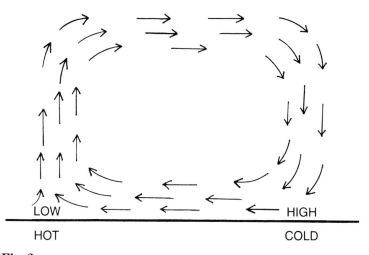

Fig 2

in the sky. Above the Arctic and Antarctic circles it does not appear above the horizon for many days in winter and in summer it circles at low altitude. This has the obvious effect of creating permanent year-round hot and low pressure conditions in the tropics and cold high pressure conditions in the polar regions.

The tendency therefore is for warm equatorial air to rise and flow as upper air to higher latitudes and for cold air to flow on the surface from polar regions to lower latitudes. Both horizontal streams of air are however being carried eastwards by the earth's rotation which movement influences the direction of flow of upper air from the equator polewards and of the lower air from the poles towards the tropics and indeed influences the direction of all free movement on the earth's surface.

The speed at which a place on the earth's surface is being carried due to the daily rotation depends upon its radius from the earth's north-south axis, which depends upon its latitude. A place on the equator has a radius of rotation equal to the radius of the earth, which is about 4,000 miles (6,437 km). To travel round the complete circumference of that radius in twenty-four hours requires a speed of little more than 1,000 miles per hour (1,610 kph). At latitude sixty degrees the radius of rotation is only half that at the equator. The speed of the place in that latitude is there-fore a little over 500 miles per hour (805 kph). At the poles the

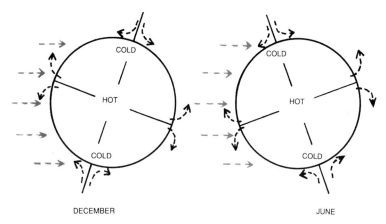

DECEMBER

JUNE

Fig 3

movement reduces to a revolving point rather like at the centre of a turn-table going round at one revolution per twenty-four hours.

Of course we are not conscious of this movement since we can only experience movement relative to the earth. If you are in a train travelling at a uniform speed, you are not conscious of moving at more than that speed when you walk towards the front of the train, nor at something less than its speed when you walk towards the rear. As long as you do not look out of the windows you are aware only of your movements relative to the train. Only when it slows or accelerates do you feel any motion and that also is relative to the train as you tend to continue as you were before the change of speed.

The same applies to movement on earth. If air is caused to move from a low latitude to a higher latitude, that is northward in the northern hemisphere and southward in the southern hemisphere, it will be moving from a surface which is in motion west to east at a speed depending on its latitude to a surface which is moving west to east at a lesser speed because of its higher latitude. The result is that it will tend to continue at its original speed and direction which will cause it to turn eastwards. This is the same reasoning as applies to the motion felt on the braking or acceleration of the train. When it brakes you fall forward as you tend to maintain the original speed and in any accelerating vehicle you feel the forward propulsion as you tend to remain behind.

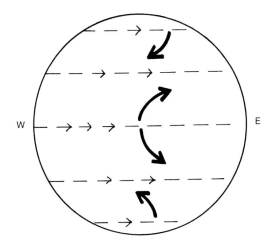

Fig 4

Similarly if air is caused to move from a high latitude to a lower latitude it will be moving towards a surface of greater west to east speed and will tend to lag behind the speed of its new surroundings, giving it a westerly movement relative to the surface. In each case it is seen that this causes the moving air to turn to the *right* in the northern hemisphere and to the *left* in the southern hemisphere.

Physicists like to see that the laws of physics are being obeyed. Newton's famous laws of motion state that a body can only change its motion if acted upon by an external force and that the change of motion will be in the direction of the force. The cause of turning to the right in north latitude and to the left in south latitude is not a direct impressed force, but in order that the movement can be followed and calculated its cause is identified as the Coriolis force, which force is of importance in dealing with winds and also with tides and ocean currents.

The explanation for the Coriolis force applied to movement starting in north south direction has been given for many years in many classrooms and nearly always there is one student who, having remained awake, asks 'What about movement starting off in an east west direction?' So, looking at air which is caused to move in an east west direction in any latitude, when at rest it is being carried round by the earth's rotation at a speed depending

15

upon its latitude. Now any body moving in a circle requires a force directed towards the centre of the circle in order to maintain the circular motion. For this force there is another name, centripetal force. This is a matter of common experience such as swinging a weight around at the end of a piece of string. The tension in the string provides the force and if it is let go the weight will fly off in a straight path. If the speed of rotation is increased the tension in the string will increase and it will lessen if the speed of rotation is reduced.

If the tension on the string is kept constant, then to increase the speed of the circling weight some extra length of string would have to be let out. In other words the radius of revolution would be increased until the speed round the wider circle is maintained by the same force. Similarly at reduced speed the string would be wound in.

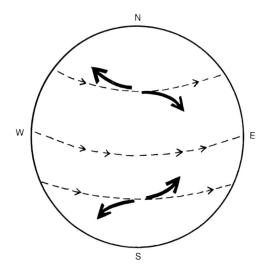

Fig 5

In the case of air on the earth's surface, gravity provides the force to the centre, the centripetal force. Air at rest in north latitude will be carried west to east at a speed depending on its latitude, that is depending on its radius of rotation. If it is caused to move east-wards relative to the surface it will now be travelling at a speed greater than that of the surface at that latitude. It will therefore tend to increase its radius of rotation. Since it is confined within a limited height it will take a southward movement nearer to the equator to a latitude of greater radius.

Similarly if air is caused to move westerly it will be travelling at a speed less than that of the earth's surface at the latitude and will tend to reduce its radius of motion and will take up a northwards movement towards a latitude of smaller radius. In each case the moving air will turn *right*.

In the south latitude the same reasoning shows that when air is caused to move eastwards it will tend to take a northwards movement and when caused to move westwards it will take up a southwards movement. In the southern hemisphere the moving air will turn to the *left*.

The Coriolis force directing movement to the right in the northern hemisphere and to the left in the southern hemisphere has its greatest effect in high latitudes, reducing in lower latitudes and disappearing at the equator. The force causing air to move on the surface from an area of high pressure to an area of low pressure is the pressure gradient force or simply the gradient force. Wind is the movement of air under the balance of the gradient force and the Coriolis force. The direction of the wind is named by the compass direction *from* which it is moving. Air moving to the east relative to the earth's surface is therefore a westerly wind; similarly air moving southwards is a northerly wind and so on.

We can now look at the general movement of air around the earth's surface resulting from these forces acting on the heated and rising equatorial air and on the cold and heavier polar air. The heated air at the equator rises and flows as an upper wind to higher latitudes. It turns right in the north and left in the south to become in each case a westerly wind. By this time in about latitude thirty degrees north and south it has cooled and sinks to the surface where it spreads out and much of it is still turning to return to the equator where it is heated and rises again. The result is that between the equatorial low and about latitude thirty degrees north the air movement on the surface is from the north-east producing what is known as the north-east trade wind. Similarly in the belt between the equatorial low and about thirty degrees south latitude the south-east trade wind prevails.

Meanwhile the cold air from the poles, flowing on the surface to lower latitudes, turns to become an easterly wind. Below about lati-

tudes sixty north and south it meets the warmer westerly wind
which has spread out from the descending equatorial air. The cold
easterly wind pushes under the warmer air which rises and turns
back to lower latitudes.

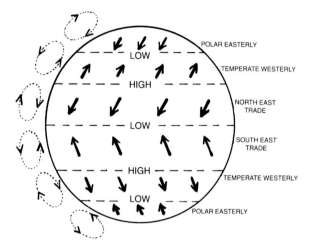

Fig 6

The trade winds converge on the equator and rise. There is thus an
equatorial convergence zone resulting in a belt of low pressure. The
upper winds flowing polewards cool and sink, building up high
pressure which is always to the right, back to wind, in north latitude
and to the left, back to wind, in south latitude. Thus there are belts
of high pressure at about latitude thirty degrees north and south.

The boundary along which the cold polar easterlies and the temperate westerlies meet is known as the polar front and lies between
latitudes forty and sixty degrees. The converging air results in a belt
of comparatively low pressure. The warm air rises over the cold air
and joins a vertical circulation of upper cooling air towards the
poles where it descends to return as the surface polar air.

The two vertical circulations set up a third between them. Some
of the warm air rising at the polar front taking an upper path
towards lower latitudes and sinking on meeting the upper equatorial air.

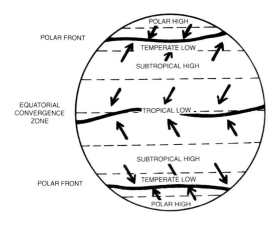

Fig 7

The overall result is –

High pressure at each polar region.

Cold easterly winds at high latitudes.

Temperate westerly winds at about latitude forty north and south. The temperate westerlies and cold easterlies meet along the polar front, a sloping boundary with cold air below and warm air above. Along the front the interaction of the warm and cold air causes changeable weather and there is a belt of low pressure.

Sub tropical high pressure between about latitudes twenty and forty degrees.

North-east and south-east trade winds between the equator and about latitudes twenty north and south.

The trade winds converge along a belt known as the equatorial convergence zone or sometimes the inter-tropical front, although it is not a front as is generally understood to describe the boundary between different types of air as at the polar front. The rising air at the equator results in an area of calms and also of heavy tropical rain.

The distribution of pressure and wind described is generally apparent around the world but is much disturbed by the unequal heating and cooling of the land and sea and the variation in the sun's heat received between summer and winter and to some extent by day and night. The variations cause comparatively little difference in the sea surface temperature as heat is absorbed through some depth of water and is circulated and distributed, so preventing fluctuations of temperature in immediate response to change in the amount of heat received.

The heat received on land is absorbed by a shallow surface which heats up quickly. Equally it loses its heat into space quickly. It therefore responds rapidly to day and night heating and cooling with corresponding change in temperature of the air above. Similarly a large land mass heats much more than the ocean in summer and is much colder than the ocean in winter.

The most marked seasonal variation is caused by the intense cooling of the vast expanse of land of the northern part of Asia in the northern winter and the intense heating of its southern part in summer. Because of this the trade wind flow is interrupted in the Indian Ocean and the China Sea. In winter the cold air flows south-wards towards the equator from the extensive high pressure over the land and joins the north-east trade wind. This is the north-east monsoon. Coming from such a land mass it has little moisture and brings the dry season to India. In summer the heated land causes extensive low pressure towards which there flows cooler air from the ocean to the south. Having come from over the ocean it con-tains a lot of moisture and as soon as it begins to rise over the heated land this is deposited as heavy rain. This is the south-west monsoon which brings the wet season.

Seasonal monsoons occur at other land masses such as Australia and South America. The effect in North America is not so great because of the unsettling influence of the warm and cold air boundary at the polar front. Africa lies across the equator and experiences less seasonal variation. These land masses do however alter the theoretical pattern of belts of high pressure and low pressure round the earth at different latitudes. The belts reduce to separate areas which prevail over the oceans, while over the land the pressure is more variable. Consequently the theoreti-cal winds prevail over the oceans with, apart from the monsoons, little seasonal variation.

The result is a large anticyclone north of the equator in the North Atlantic and the same in the North Pacific. These are the sub-tropical highs which tend to move further north and intensify in summer bringing to higher latitudes the temperate westerly winds and consequently the polar front. In each case there is low pressure to the north, which areas are pushed further north in

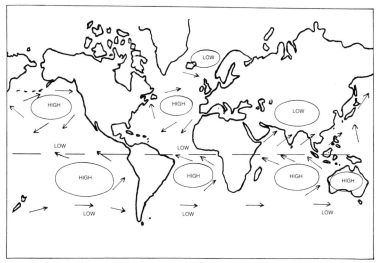

PRESSURE and WIND   JULY

Fig 8

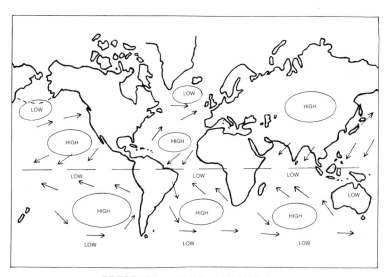

PRESSURE and WIND   JANUARY

Fig 9

21

summer. In winter the areas of high pressure generally subside to some extent allowing the low pressure areas to drift south and have greater influence on the weather of the temperate latitudes. The pressure over Asia alternates between high and low with winter and summer.

In the southern hemisphere there is a great expanse of continuous ocean and not so much change in the areas of high pressure in the South Atlantic and South Pacific and there is a similar anticyclonic area in the South Indian Ocean. Over Australia pressure is high in the southern winter and low in the summer causing some change in the wind circulation there. This is mainly a reduction in the south-east trade wind in summer. At the same time the northeast trade wind, augmented by the north-east monsoon, continues right across the equator from the northern hemisphere and can turn to appear from the north-west before meeting the south-east trades.

Isobars and the Wind

The traditional method of measuring atmospheric pressure is by measuring the length of a column of mercury which the pressure of air can support. A simple mercury barometer is made by filling a glass tube, closed at one end, with mercury and turning it upside down with its open end inserted in a basin of mercury. The mercury in the tube takes up a level depending upon the atmospheric pressure acting on the surface in the basin. The space between the top of the tube and the mercury is now a vacuum and exerts no pressure. The length of the mercury column can be measured in inches or in centimetres. The average reading at sea-level is about thirty inches or seventy-six centimetres.

Changes in atmospheric pressure can be indicated by the expansion and contraction of a flexible chamber which has been partially exhausted of air. The movement of the wall of the chamber in response to increase and decrease in pressure is conveyed through sensitive mechanism to a pointer moving over a graduated dial. This is the aneroid barometer which is popular and convenient for measuring rise and fall of pressure and so giving some indication of approaching weather.

A record of change of pressure is obtained from a barograph. The movement of the chamber wall is conveyed by a lever system

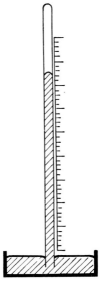

Simple Barometer

Fig 10

to a pen. The pen touches a graduated chart placed round a revolving drum which makes one revolution every twenty-four hours. By this means the barometric tendency is seen at a glance at the trace of the chart, that is, whether the pressure is rising or falling and if so how rapidly.

The precision aneroid barometer has been developed from the basic instrument. Refinements in sensitivity and mechanism and the use of electronic circuitry allow precise readings. The instrument has replaced the specially constructed mercury barometer previously used for accurate measurement at sea which was known as the Kew Pattern Marine Barometer.

Pressure is defined as force per unit area. While inches or centimetres of mercury provide for recognition of changes in pressure, for meteorological work a standard unit of pressure is required. The unit is the bar, which is divided into thousandths named *millibars*. It is in millibars that atmospheric pressure is measured and recorded. A bar or one thousand millibars is equal to a pressure of seventy-five centimetres of mercury which is just

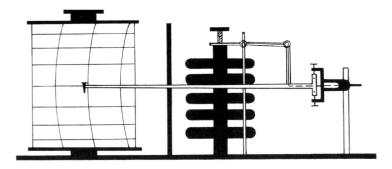

Barograph

Fig 11

a little less than the average pressure at sea-level in temperate latitudes.

Since the atmospheric pressure at any place is the weight of air above, pressure must decrease with height. The rate of decrease is about one millibar per ten metres near the ground and as we go higher the rate becomes less since the atmosphere becomes less dense with altitude. In order that pressure readings at places of differing height above sea-level may be compared, they are each adjusted to the corresponding sea-level reading. In other words all readings are corrected for height above sea-level.

Having given a number of barometric readings taken at the same time in different places and corrected for height above sea-level, lines drawn on a map or chart, through places of equal readings will indicate the distribution of pressure and the pressure gradient that prevails. These lines are *isobars*. Such readings, among other observations, are made at regular intervals at weather stations throughout the world. Ships at sea make important contributions in this respect, since the greater part of the earth's surface is deep sea.

Isobars are usually drawn at four millibar intervals, but on large scale charts at two millibar intervals. In most cases the isobars will be found to form closed curves around centres of low pressure or round areas of high pressure, although the area being mapped may not be extensive enough to show the totally enclosed curve and the centre around which it is curving may be off the map. The distance between adjacent isobars is an indication of the pressure gradient at the place. Where the isobars are close together there is a steep difference in pressure and therefore a strong pressure gradient force tending to propel the air from the high pressure area to the low pressure area. Conversely when the isobars are widely spaced there is less tendency for the air to flow. It follows that closely spaced isobars indicate strong winds and widely spaced isobars indicate light winds.

The gradient force is in effect the force of gravity causing the air to fall from high pressure to low pressure somewhat as it might flow down the gradient of a mountainside. Tending to move towards the low it is acted upon by the Coriolis force which in the northern hemisphere causes it to turn to the right. It will continue to turn to the right until it attains a balance of movement under the forces acting upon it. In the absence of any other forces that would be under the balance of the gradient force to the left and the Coriolis force to the right.

The resultant theoretical wind is known as the *geostrophic* wind. It is sometimes referred to simply as the gradient wind which name is convenient so long as it is understood that it is not in the direction of the gradient force but is parallel to the isobars.

Air moving over the ground suffers a frictional effect which retards its motion. This additional force causes the moving air to reach a balanced flow in a direction inclined towards the centre of low pressure. The inclination is greatest at ground level and at about the height of low cloud the frictional effect will disappear and the wind flows more nearly parallel to the isobars. Over the sea surface the wind is not so restricted by friction and the wind direction is close to the geostrophic direction.

The wind thus flows around a centre of low pressure in an anti-clockwise direction in the northern hemisphere and in a clock-wise direction in the southern hemisphere. At ground level the flow is inclined towards the centre, the inclination being greater over land than sea.

By the same reasoning it will be seen that the wind flows around a centre of high pressure in a clockwise direction in the northern hemisphere and in an anti-clockwise direction in the southern hemisphere. The inclination from the direction of the isobars is outwards from the centre, again greater over land than over the

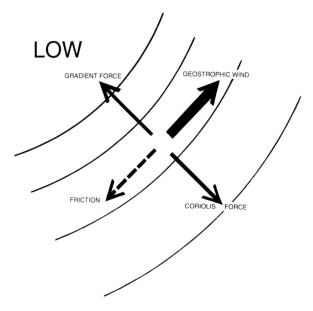

Fig 12

sea. An area of low pressure is named a *depression* or simply a *LOW*. An area of high pressure is named an *anticyclone* or simply a *HIGH*.

A depression is caused by warm air rising in cooler surroundings. Surrounding air flows in to replace the rising air and if there is a continuing source feeding the warmer air the process will continue and intensify. The source may be some local heating or more generally the continuing inflow of warmer air into the colder air as can take place at the polar front. In any case the inflowing air has to rise and as it rises it cools. Being comparatively warm, it has a high water vapour content and soon the cooling condenses the vapour to form cloud. As the condensation grows it forms drops which fall as rain. A depression is thus associated with overcast skies and rain and, particularly in winter when cold air pushing to lower latitudes can have its lowest temperature, the system often intensifies and depressions are associated with stormy and severe weather.

In a high pressure area the air is descending and flowing outwards. The cause is not localised and the movement is not violent.

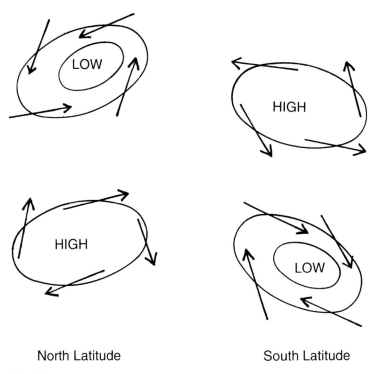

North Latitude   South Latitude

Fig 13

The descending air is usually heated and becomes drier with no tendency to produce cloud. It is only when some local pocket of rising air is encountered that small isolated clouds may appear. An anticyclone is thus associated with dry clear weather. Sometimes as in winter when the ground has lost heat, the descending air may meet a cooler level and a blanket of cloud may form. This sometimes gives dull, gloomy and dry winter anticyclonic conditions.

The changing atmospheric pressure gives rise to moving patterns of isobars and as they move, a change of wind and weather is experienced. High pressure may push between lows, usually from the equatorial side. The isobars of a low may extend in one direction forming a V shape at which the wind may alter direction abruptly and weather may be more severe. This is usually towards the equator and along a zone between warmer and colder air.

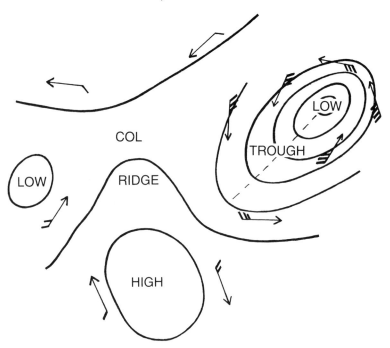

Fig 14

An area of no pressure gradient and therefore of calms, between depressions and anticyclones is known as a *col*. An extension of isobars round a high is a *ridge*. These features are analogous to the cols, ridges and valleys of mountainous terrain.

Wind direction is normally shown by means of 'arrows' pointing in the direction in which the air is moving. A small circle at the head of an arrow marks the position where the wind force and direction was observed. The 'feathers' at the tail of the arrow indicate wind speed. Wind speed at sea is usually reported using the Beaufort Scale which is described later. The feathers drawn on the left of the arrow correspond to the Beaufort force figure. Wind speed may sometimes be reported in knots or in miles per hour or kilometres per hour. One knot is equal to about 1.15 mph or 1.85 kph.

The wind direction shown by the arrows in Figure 14 are as might be expected in the northern hemisphere. It will be seen that when facing in the direction in which the arrow is pointing in each case atmospheric pressure is lower on the left hand and higher on the right. The opposite would be the case in the southern hemisphere. A statement of this is made by Buys Ballot's Law which is that if you stand with your back to the wind, the lower pressure lies to your left in the northern hemisphere and to your right in the southern hemisphere.

The strongest winds are experienced where the isobars are closest. This is generally around a depression as shown. The col is an area of variable light winds between opposing wind directions. In a trough of low pressure the wind can be in strong gusts and squalls under a band of thick cloud and rain. In a ridge of high pressure the wind is directional but light.

Since wind flows in response to the pressure gradient, the velocity of the geostrophic wind can be calculated from measurement of the distance between adjacent isobars at two or four millibar intervals. This wind is the result of the Coriolis force and the pressure gradient. The Coriolis force depends upon the latitude and is least near the equator and greater in the higher latitudes. The measure of distance between the isobars must therefore be adjusted for latitude. In practice a scale is used which has graduations varying with latitude. This is placed across the isobars and a theoretical wind speed read. This is the speed of the wind parallel to the isobars without frictional effect. At sea this is usually close to the actual wind experienced. Such a measurement from a prognostic chart can give a reasonable forecast of the wind to be expected.

Practical measurement of wind is made by the anemometer. The most common type is the 'cup' anemometer consisting usually of three arms fitted horizontally to a vertical spindle. The arms equally angled 120° apart each carry a hemispherical cup at the outer end. This is mounted to revolve horizontally with minimum friction and calibrated so that the speed of rotation is a measure of the wind speed. The rate of rotation may be transmitted mechanically or electrically to a display indicating wind speed in knots or other units. A wind vane is usually fitted to point into the wind, the direction of which may also be transmitted to the display.

Because of its rotational momentum the cup anemometer does not give an instantaneous reading of changes in wind speed as in

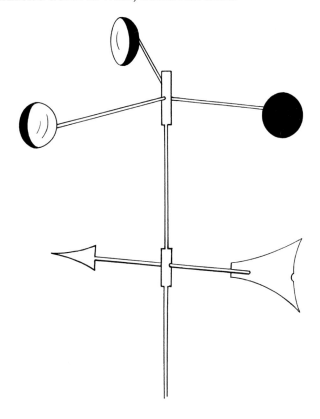

ANEMOMETER

Fig 15

sudden gusts. One method of obtaining measure of gustiness of the wind is to mount an open ended tube as a wind vane so that the open end faces the wind. The pressure set up in the tube fluctuates with the gusts which are electrically transmitted to a tracing pen. Another method is to fit a small propeller on the wind-facing end of a weather vane. The wind actuates the propeller, the rate of rotation of which is recorded.

On a vessel at sea, the wind vane will indicate the wind direction and speed actually experienced on board. This is the *apparent wind* which is the resultant of the true wind and the vessel's

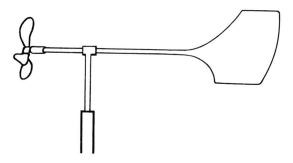

WIND SPEED RECORDER

Fig 16

course and speed. In some cases there is provision for feeding these factors into the instrument and a correction is made automatically so that the true wind strength and direction is displayed. Otherwise the true wind is found by simple plotting. A straight line is drawn in direction and length representing the vessel's course and speed. From the starting point of the course line and using the same scale, a line is drawn in the direction of the apparent wind and of length representing the apparent wind speed. Complete the triangle and the third side represents the true wind in speed and direction. The wind vane reading will normally indicate direction relative to the ship's head. The vessel's course and speed can conventionally be drawn in the 'ships head up' direction.

For example (Fig 17a) in a vessel speed of 12 knots the apparent wind is 45° on the starboard bow (Right or Green or Starboard 045°) at 20 knots. The straight line AB of length 12 convenient units represents the vessel's course and speed. The line AC drawn 45° to the right of length 20 of the same units represents the apparent wind. The third side BC is found to be 80° to the right and of length 14 units. The true wind is therefore 80° on the starboard bow (Right or Green or Starboard 080°) at 14 knots. If for example, the ship's head is East, the wind is South by East.

In Figure 17b the vessel's speed is 7 knots and the apparent wind 45° on the port quarter (Left or Red or Port135°) at 10 knots. The apparent wind line is drawn at 45° from line astern. The third side is found to be at an angle of 28° from line astern and of length 16

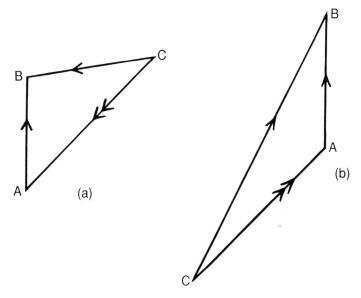

Fig 17

units. The true wind is therefore 28° on the port quarter (Left or Red or Port 152°) at 16 knots. If as before the ship's head is East, the true wind is West North West.

Beaufort Scale of Wind Force

The Beaufort Scale provides a convenient way of describing and reporting the force or speed of the wind. The name is that of the Admiral who first devised a scale in 1805, in which he identified the wind force by the amount of sail a square-rigged ship could carry. With the demise of the square-riggers, the sea surface itself was seen as a readily available indicator of the force of the wind. The scale was then amended to make use of the state of the sea as a criterion.

The scale is simply a means of reporting wind force in classes from calm to hurricane numbered zero to twelve. If the observer has no instrumental means of measuring the force of the wind, then the sea surface criteria is used. This requires personal judgement which can only be acquired by experience and which may be gained over a period of observation of various states of sea relating to known wind speed. The true wind force is thus estimated and the direction of the waves provides indication of true wind direction.

The scale is given in the table. The units of wind force are usually represented by the tail feathers of the wind arrows on a weather map. Half a feather corresponds to one unit of force. One feather represents force 2. Two and a half feathers represents force 5 and so on.

Beaufort Scale of Wind Force

Beaufort Scale Number	Wind Speed in knots	General Description of wind	Description of sea
0	less than 1	Calm	Flat calm
1	1–3	Light air.	Ripples
2	4–6	Light breeze.	Small glassy wavelets
3	7–10	Gentle breeze.	Wavelets with slight crests
4	11–16	Moderate breeze.	Small waves, frequent white crests
5	17–21	Fresh breeze.	Moderate waves, many white crests
6	22–28	Strong breeze.	Waves having white crests everywhere
7	29–33	Near gale.	Wave crests blown off in streaks
8	34–40	Gale.	Wave crests breaking into spindrift
9	41–47	Strong gale.	High waves with dense streaks of foam
10	48–55	Storm.	Very high waves with long streaks of foam
11	56–63	Violent storm.	Exceptionally high waves with long patches of foam
12	over 63	Hurricane.	Sea completely covered with foam and driving spray

Air Masses

An air mass might be defined as an extensive volume of air having generally uniform temperature and moisture content. Its temperature and moisture content is not necessarily constant and usually undergoes change but there are no sudden contrasts. There are two basic air mass types. Warm air originating in the tropical regions and cold air originating in polar regions.

Polar air coming into lower latitude is heated at ground level and there is rapid fall in temperature with height. In other words it has a large environmental lapse rate. Air which is caused to rise, as we have seen, cools at a constant rate due to fall in pressure and expansion. That is at the adiabatic rate which in polar air is for the most part less than the environmental rate. It goes on rising and when cloud is formed it is built up vertically often producing showers and squalls. Polar air is thus generally unstable.

Tropical air going into higher latitude has much less temperature fall with height and might be cooled at ground level in which case there is a rise in temperature above ground. Its environmental lapse rate is small and might even be reversed near the ground. Any rising air which will be cooling more rapidly at the adiabatic rate soon stops rising. When cloud is formed it is spread horizontally, its only movement is its turbulence within the cloud layer. Tropical air is thus generally stable.

There are thus two general types of air mass. Polar air has the characteristics of instability, building up large vertical cloud with turbulence throughout the cloud height. This type of cloud is named Cumulus and is frequently associated with showers and squalls. In mild weather the same cloud type is seen as white rounded cloud with a flat base drifting in a blue sky. Tropical air has the characteristics of stability with its cloud in layers. This type of cloud is named Stratus. It can form at various levels and is often low in humid conditions and often the cloud does not get off the ground, giving mist and poor visibility.

The type of weather experienced in either air mass will depend much upon its water content. The characteristics of both polar and tropical air masses are influenced by the area over which they have travelled from source. If the air has travelled over the ocean it will have picked up moisture. Air from over land is named *continental* and air from over water is named *maritime*. Polar air having travelled over land is named *polar continental* and from over the ocean it is *polar maritime*. Similarly there is *tropical continental* and *tropical maritime*.

Thus we have four main types of air mass:

Polar continental – Cold and dry
Polar maritime – Cold and moist
Tropical continental – Warm and dry
Tropical maritime – Warm and moist

The characteristics of each are determined by their source and their travel. Polar air which is direct from the ice capped Arctic regions is differentiated by naming it *arctic air* and air directly from the equatorial convergence belt is differentiated by naming it *equatorial air*.

Generally in temperate latitudes low pressure systems keep on the move and the weather is changeable. Anticyclonic systems can persist for longer periods and can establish the flow of a particular air mass with associated spells of weather. As experienced in Northern Europe these may be generalised as follows.

Polar Continental

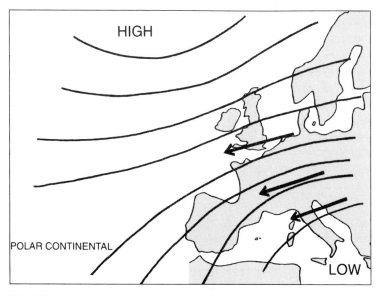

Fig 18

Under the influence of an anticyclone north of the British Isles or over Scandinavia the air stream is polar continental. It winter it can be very cold and although dry with clear skies over mainland Europe it can pick up enough moisture from the Baltic and North Seas to produce heavy falls of snow in Britain. In summer the polar air, having passed over a warm land mass, loses much of its polar characteristics and usually gives stable conditions. Again it is dry until meeting the Baltic and North Seas and the moisture gained over them may produce fog.

Polar Maritime

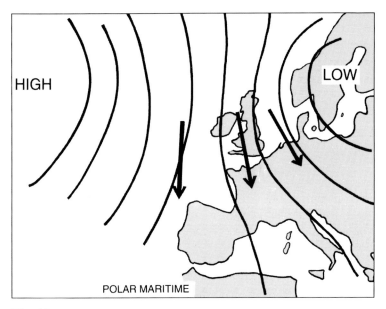

Fig 19

Under the influence of an anticyclone north-west of the British Isles and with low pressure to the east, the air flow is polar maritime. It may be due north from Arctic regions or north-west from Greenland and the northern regions of Canada. Heavy rain and hail showers may be experienced and possibly snow if from the north. From over the North Atlantic strong gales are frequent. Similar gales and showers may be experienced in summer but less fierce and less cold.

Tropical Continental

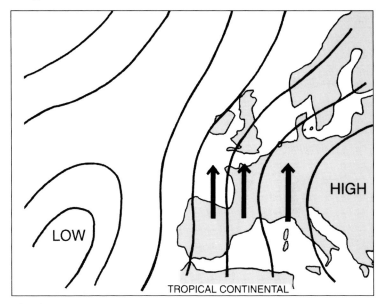

Fig 20

With an anticyclone over Eastern Europe and low pressure to the west, tropical continental air comes from North Africa. It is dry and hot producing heat-wave conditions in summer. In winter it is cooled to some extent on reaching the colder European continent.

Tropical Maritime

When the sub-tropical high pressure area in the Atlantic north of the equator pushes north to bring in tropical maritime air, the westerly flow to Northern Europe is warm and moist. It is cooled as it meets the colder more northerly water and its moisture is condensed to produce low cloud, drizzle and fog. This is much the same in summer and winter. After crossing the land it may dry out to give clearer conditions in the eastern part of Europe.

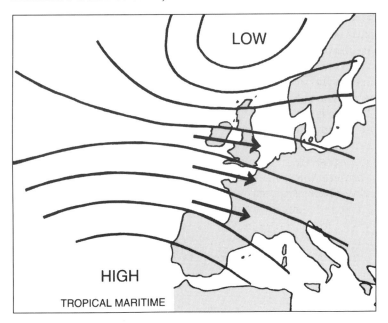

Fig 21

Fronts and Depressions

Where a cold air mass and a warm air mass meet they do not gently intermingle to form a lukewarm airmass. Rather like oil and water, the less dense and lighter warm air floats above the denser and heavier air along a sloping boundary which is called a front. A front is rarely tranquil. Differences in pressure and in wind direction and velocity cause disturbance along the front and differences in temperature and moisture content develop cloud and rain.

In both the north and south hemispheres warm air from the subtropical highs and cold polar air meet as competing air masses in the temperate latitudes. The front along which they meet is a polar front. There the two air masses converge. Converging air is forced upwards exerting less pressure on the surface and, mixing along this turbulent front, depressions are developed which travel along in the prevailing westerly flow, causing the changeable weather found in these latitudes. Changing wind direction, rain and showers, together with calms and ridges of high pressure between are the familiar weather features of a polar front.

Since prevailing pressure systems are more defined over the oceans than over the land, the consequent air flow is more persistent over the oceans. The polar front lying across the North Atlantic is always present somewhere, generally pushed north in the summer and drifting to lower latitudes in the winter, producing the depressions which develop over the ocean and travel north-easterly to affect the British Isles and Northern Europe. Northern America is similarly but less affected from the Pacific. In winter North America can have its own polar front across the continent and joining the North Atlantic front. In the southern hemisphere fronts appear in all three southern oceans affecting South America, South Africa and Australia.

In the Mediterranean, mainly in winter, there is a frontal zone between the warm air from North Africa and the cold air of Europe which gives rise to Mediterranean depressions. At about the equator there is a frontal zone between the north-east and south-east trade winds. In this case there is little difference between the temperature and moisture content of the two converging air masses. The zone between them is therefore not strictly a front and is generally named the equatorial convergence zone, although it is sometimes referred to as the inter-tropical front. The converging and rising air results in a belt of calms of high temperature in which deep depressions develop causing the violent tropical revolving storms.

The polar front is actually a narrow zone of transition between the weather characteristics of the two air masses. Only in that narrow frontal space is there a mixing of the two which gives rise to unstable and changeable conditions in which separate individual depressions are formed. In the mixing along the frontal zone there is a wave motion and when a wave of warm air enters the cold air there is a local reduction in pressure setting up a converging circulation. The centre of the circulation is at the tip of the wave which normally travels eastwards.

The situation in north latitude at the earth's surface is as in Fig 22. The wave of warm air is the warm sector of the depression. At the leading surface of the wave, warm air is rising above the cold air. At the rear surface, cold air is pushing under the warm air.

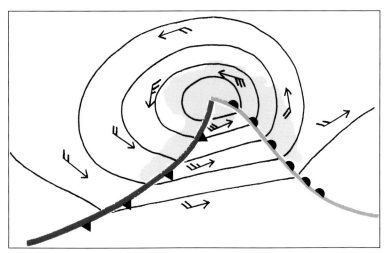

Fig 22

These two surfaces are *weather fronts*. In the lead is the *warm front* and in the rear follows the *cold front*. Across each front there is a change in the direction of the isobars and consequently a change in the direction of the wind at the passage of the weather front.

Fig 23

At the sloping boundaries the water vapour content of the warm air is condensed, forming cloud and rain. The cloud and rainfall experienced at that stage of the depression is illustrated in Figure 23. The long sloping warm front produces continuous cloud and rain. The more vertical cold front produces more vertical cloud

40

and rain is possibly heavier but for shorter periods. Winds follow the direction of the isobars, changing clockwise at each front.

As the central area of low pressure continues to develop, the cold front advances more rapidly than the warm front, catching up with it at first at the centre of the low, then progressively along its length. As the two fronts meet they are said to be *occluded*. They, then form a single occluded front.

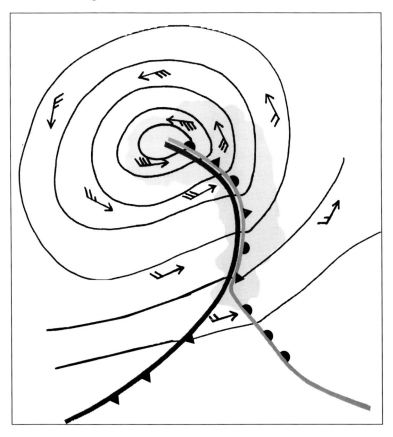

Fig 24

At this stage the depression appears as in Figure 24. The occlusion lifts the warm sector off the ground. The warm front weather and the cold front weather then meet and there is an abrupt change in wind direction. Usually when occlusion takes place, the advancing cold air lifts the warm front as shown in Figure 25. This is a cold occlusion. If the polar air in front of the depression is colder than that behind, as when polar continental air has been coming in from the north, the cold front may be lifted over the warm front which is a warm occlusion.

The occluded front slows down and dissolves. The circling air fills up to become a homogenous mass again on the cold side of the frontal zone.

Fig 25

Further depressions often form along the trailing cold front behind an occluded depression. These may advance rapidly and sometimes become deeper with stronger winds than the first. A chain of depressions is not uncommon. The sequence of development is illustrated in Figure 26.

In the North Atlantic the centres of depressions usually pass in a north-eastward direction to the north of the British Isles although in winter they can be well to the south. Indeed there is no regular seasonal movement and month to month irregular movement of the frontal zone is common. The weather experience however, is generally that of the southern part of a depression.

On the approach of a depression there is a southerly wind with feathery cloud named cirrus high in the sky. As the warm front approaches the cloud lowers and thickens to a ragged overcast sky. Light rain at first becomes heavier and the wind force increases. Throughout this time the barometer has been falling. At the front the barometer steadies and the wind veers to the west. In the warm sector it is mild and misty with patchy low cloud and possibly drizzle and light rain.

Fig 26

The passage of the cold front is marked by a drop in temperature, some clearance of the sky, a sharp veering of the wind to the north-west and the barometer begins to rise. There may be heavy showers from thick vertical cloud and possibly blue sky between. Strong or gale force winds with heavy squalls may accompany the showers. At an occluded front, the sequence of weather is directly from that of the approach of a warm front to that of the cold front passage without the intervening warm sector. The sequence of weather is generally more pronounced in winter and possibly quite mild in summer.

When another depression follows, the northerly wind and rising barometer in the rear of one depression soon gives way to a short calm, then falling barometer and southerly wind with the gathering veil of thin cloud, at first high in the sky, heralds the approach of the next one.

Depressions can form within air masses away from a frontal zone. Non-frontal depressions are caused by local ground heat conveyed to air and reducing pressure, such as rising air over heated land. They are more significant when caused by polar air passing over warm seas. Heated land tends to cool at night whereas warm sea tends to retain its heat and the more persistent heat causes depressions to develop. Continued activity of this type of depression owes much to the release of energy when the water vapour in the rising air is condensed into cloud. It is well known that to vaporize water, heat needs to be supplied, as in boiling. This is latent heat which does not raise the temperature but is used in altering the state. Conversely when water vapour is changed into visible drops of water as cloud, energy is released which passes to the system giving momentum to the wind circulation.

Tropical Storms

The north-east and south-east trade winds flow towards the equator where they converge and rise along the inter-tropical convergence zone, forming a band of calm surface conditions commonly known as the Doldrums. The zone encircles the globe generally following the sun's annual displacement north and south of the equator. Along this zone the sea surface can reach very high temperatures causing pockets of accelerated rising air and producing thick vertically-developing cloud, often with torrential rain and thunderstorms. At the equator there is no Coriolis force and no tendency to set up rotation of the rising air. A few degrees of latitude away from the equator however, the force is sufficient to initiate circulation.

Within about ten degrees north and south of the equator, after the sun has reached its maximum north or south declination, that is latitude, of its daily path, the sea is at its warmest. A local lowering of pressure is enough to set up a circulation in which the rising moist air condenses on a vast scale, imparting energy to develop the depression to intense depth. The periods when depressions of this kind develop are August to October in north latitude and January to March in south latitude. These depressions are much smaller in area than those of temperate latitudes but the pressure gradient is much steeper and hence the wind and weather much more fierce.

North of the equator in the Atlantic where these storms are

named Hurricanes, and in the Pacific where they are called Typhoons, they form about mid-ocean and travel westwards, curving north and north-east. In the Atlantic they curve over the West Indies and to the east coast of the USA. Over land however, they lose energy. Some may appear west of central America and travel north-west. Those originating mid to west Pacific follow a path similar to those in the Atlantic, but towards the Philippines and to the China Sea and to Japan. In the Indian Ocean they are named Cyclones, north of the equator they travel on various paths in the Bay of Bengal and Arabian Sea and south of the equator they move westwards curving south by Madagascar or, originating in the Timor Sea, they go southwards by the west coast of Australia. In the south Pacific they travel westwards and curve south by the east coast of Australia. It is a feature of the convergence zone that in the Atlantic it never moves far enough into south latitude to gain the circulating force of the Coriolis effect and consequently tropical storms do not occur in the South Atlantic.

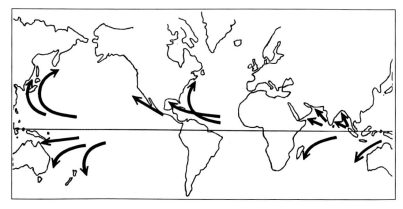

Fig 27

When near the centre of a tropical storm, the wind can be extremely fierce and the sea violent and confused. At the centre there is an area within the circling wind which may be less than ten miles in diameter. There is usually a patch of clear sky due to air sucked in from above into this central 'eye' of the storm. All round however, the violent winds are spiralling upwards producing thick dark cloud and violent rain.

There has been much research and hypothesis about the formation of tropical revolving storms. The mariner in a vessel in the vicinity of one of these is not so concerned about the theory of its origin, as he is about how to avoid the worst of its weather.

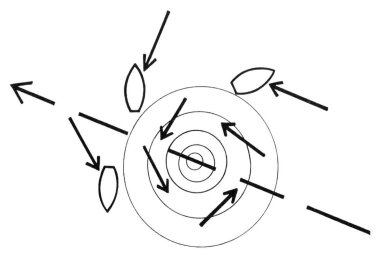

Fig 28

The weather of a tropical storm can be first experienced up to two hundred miles from its centre. Signs of the storm would be the appearance of waves in the form of swell, falling barometer, increasing cloud and wind. No doubt radio warning would already be received. The bearing of the centre of the system may be judged by Buy Ballot's law. In the northern hemisphere with back to wind the centre is on your left. Having in mind the probable path of advance and of the curvature of the path of the storm, a good estimate may be made of one's position relative to the centre. A vessel that is anywhere in front of an approaching storm or on the side towards which it may be curving will obviously wish to remove itself from the storm's path. That would be to head off with the wind in the starboard bow if to the right of the path and to run with the wind on the starboard quarter if to the left of the approaching storm. In the southern hemisphere everything is reversed. To the left of the path you head off with the wind on the port bow and to the right you run off with the wind on the port quarter. (Fig 28)

Waterspouts and Tornadoes

These are short-lived and small in area, but are violent wind circulations seen as waterspouts at sea. They usually appear as a column emerging from the base of a heavy rain and squall cloud, sucking up the air through a spiralling vortex. When the base touches the sea surface dense spray is drawn up into the funnel. These can travel quite fast and the twirling column of rain and spray advancing across the sea surface can be a spectacular sight to the viewer on board.

Over land these are Tornadoes and can be of great concentrated intensity and cause much damage along the narrow path over which they travel. This is caused by the very sudden decrease in pressure at the centre as well as by the violent wind. Dust and debris can be sucked up and accompanied by torrential rain and possibly thunder and lightning. They are short lived however, lasting at most some hours and travelling only a few miles.

Local Winds

Sea Breezes

In conditions of clear or partially clear skies and light winds, an onshore wind can be experienced which can sometimes become quite strong in the afternoon. As the sun gets up and the land heats, the air over the land is heated and rises and pressure falls relative to that over the sea. A gradient is set up which can override any existing weaker gradient and the wind blows inland. As the localised gradient tends to encircle the lower pressure over the land, the onshore wind will tend to follow the direction of the localised isobars and as the day goes on it may turn to a direction more parallel to the coast.

The rising air over the land and the descending air over the sea causes the upper air to flow from land to sea. Over land the rising air can cause cloud to develop while the descending air at sea will disperse any cloud. This leaves clear blue sky at sea while there may be a band of cloud over the land. The sea breeze calms down after sunset when the land loses its heat by radiation into space. This will happen quickly if there is no reflecting cloud cover.

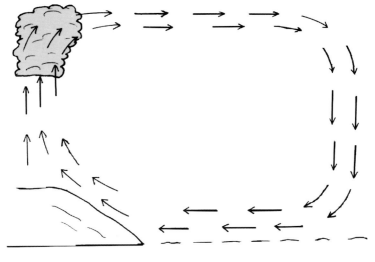

Sea Breeze

Fig 29

Winds off the land

In the circumstances of the afternoon sea breeze, once the sun has gone down the land may cool sufficiently below the sea surface temperature to set up the reverse effect. This causes a night and early morning breeze from land to sea which is less defined than the sea breeze of the day but often the sinking colder air on the land is caused to flow down hills and through valleys and is accelerated out to sea for some distance.

Wind flowing out to sea from mountains and valleys is a feature of many coasts. When a flow of wind is obstructed by a mountain range it piles up on the windward side and is funnelled through the gaps and down valleys which causes it to be accelerated to sometimes gale force. One well known example is the Mistral in the Mediterranean, coming from the Rhône Valley in the south of France. The Mediterranean is geographically inviting to such winds of which there are many around its coasts.

When wind is forced up and over a mountain range it descends on the lee side as a dry warm wind. This is known as the Föhn or Foehn effect. On being forced up the mountain, it is cooled at the adiabatic rate which depends on its water content. Moisture is

48

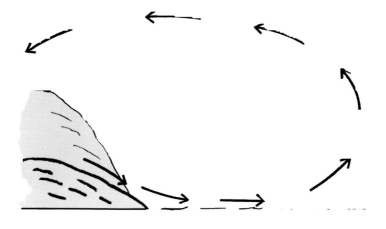

Off Land Wind

Fig 30

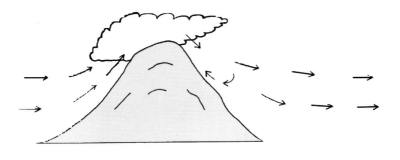

Föhn Wind

Fig 31

condensed to cloud and rain. On descending it is heated, also at the adiabatic rate which, because it is now dry, is greater than its cooling rate on ascending. Consequently it returns to the horizontal rather warmer than when it started on the windward side. Such a down sweeping wind going out to sea can be experienced off any mountainous coast.

Wind blowing off a high steep shore will not descend smoothly but may set up a vertical circulation and possibly a reversal of the wind direction near the shore.

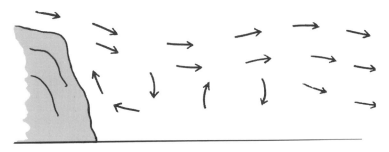

Fig 32

An apparently sheltered anchorage with high land all round can often be uncomfortable. The effect of wind funnelling down valleys and the turbulence of wind coming down mountainsides can cause strong winds, calms and gusts which result in yawing and swinging at anchor.

Coastal Winds

We have seen that surface wind blows nearly parallel to the isobars over the sea and over the land and that due to frictional drag it inclines towards the low pressure. In the northern hemisphere the low is to the left with back to wind, so over land the wind is inclined more to the left of its isobar direction than wind over the sea. The result is that winds blowing along a coastline may be found to diverge, causing a coastal calm belt, or may converge causing a belt of rougher weather depending upon the side on which the land lies. For example in the northern hemisphere a west wind blowing along a coast to the north will continue west at sea and will angle towards north over the land. The wind will thus diverge along the coast and there will be less wind inshore than found out at sea. Divergence causes subsiding air and consequently there is less likelihood of cloud along the south-facing shore in a westerly wind.

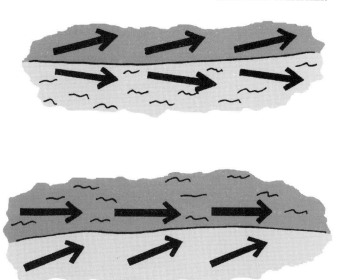

Fig 33

The same wind blowing along a coast to the south will also continue west at sea and angle to the north over the land, which in this case will cause convergence. This will cause stronger winds near the coast. Convergence causes rising air and there is more likelihood of cloud in the same conditions along a north-facing shore. An easterly wind will have the opposite effect while in the southern hemisphere each situation will be reversed.

Winds at any angle to the shoreline suffer deflection due to the difference in friction effect at sea and over land. Wind from land to sea is deflected away from the low pressure side on meeting the sea. In the northern hemisphere the low pressure is on the left so wind from land always veers to the right off-shore. By the same reasoning wind from the sea to land inclines to the left inland but this is of less concern to the mariner. As usual the opposite is the case in the southern hemisphere.

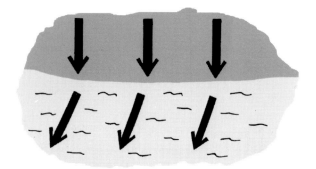

Fig 34

Winds along a shore are increased round a headland. This is due to the funnelling effect causing divergence round the headland. A slight to moderate sea along the coast can become quite rough as the headland is rounded. This is accentuated because there is a similar effect on the waves themselves.

Fig 35

Wind can similarly be funnelled through narrow straits. An example of this is the Levanter, a strong easterly wind which can be met on approaching the Straits of Gibraltar from the Atlantic. A west wind can be accelerated in the same way to be met on approaching the Straits from the Mediterranean.

CHAPTER 2

Cloud and Fog

The evaporation of water is the process of its change from liquid to vapour. Water vapour is invisible and is always present in the air. The reverse process from water vapour to water is condensation. When the water vapour in the air is condensed it becomes visible as cloud, fog or mist.

Evaporation takes place from a water surface into the air with which it is in contact and may be visualised as molecules of water escaping into the air. Warm air can accept more water vapour than cold air. At some point the air will have absorbed all the vapour it can hold. It is then saturated. At that point a drop in temperature will cause the vapour to condense into visible water droplets suspended in the air. At the same point a rise in temperature will allow further evaporation to take place. The temperature at which the air becomes saturated is its *dew point*. The amount of water vapour in the air is its *humidity*. This is quantified in percentage terms as the ratio of the amount of vapour in the air relative to the amount required for saturation and is named *relative humidity*.

An indication of the relative humidity of the air may be obtained from the reading of two thermometers. One thermometer simply reads the temperature of the air. The bulb of the other is kept moist, usually by having it wrapped in a piece of material kept wet by soaking up water from a small reservoir. This is known as the wet bulb and the other the dry bulb. Evaporation takes place from the wet bulb at a rate depending upon the dryness of the air. The change of state from water to water vapour requires an absorption of heat which is the latent heat of evaporation. The removal of this heat at the wet bulb causes the thermometer to register a temperature lower than that shown on the dry bulb. The difference is known as the depression of the wet bulb and is maximum when the air is very dry, allowing maximum evaporation. It is zero when no evaporation takes place, that is when the air is saturated.

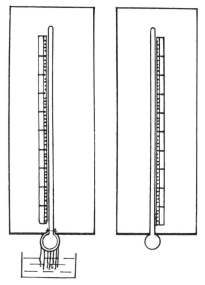

Wet and Dry Bulb Hygrometer

Fig 36

The depression of the wet bulb is therefore a measure of the relative humidity. When both thermometers read the same, the relative humidity is 100% and the temperature shown is the dew point. At any other temperature the relative humidity can be calculated from the readings. When required it is usually obtained from pre-calculated tables but for ordinary purposes the depression of the wet bulb is sufficient information.

The two thermometers may be mounted in a screened box allowing a free current of air to pass through or they may be mounted in a frame arranged so that it can be whirled round by hand. A humidity measuring instrument is named a hygrometer. The wet and dry bulb instrument may be more precisely named a psychrometer. There are other types of hygrometer, the most common being the hair hygrometer which makes use of the property of hair to increase in length in moist conditions and to contract in dry conditions. The expansion and contraction can be conveyed to a marker making a trace on paper on a revolving drum, thus giving a continuous record of relative humidity.

When air is cooled below its dew point the excess water vapour condenses to form mist, fog or cloud. When cooled by contact with a surface the condensation is in the form of dew and when below freezing point, hoar frost. There can be conditions when in very clear air, condensation does not take place until the temperature is well below dew point. This is because condensation occurs most readily on minute particles of dust or matter in the air and in the absence of such particles the formation of water drops is delayed. The air is then said to be supersaturated.

Cloud is formed generally when rising air reaches a level at which it is cooled below its dew point. Rising air expands because atmospheric pressure decreases with height. Expansion uses up heat and since no heat is being imparted the air cools. This adiabatic cooling as already described. At its dew point condensation will begin and cloud is formed. This will occur at a certain height which is seen as the cloud base.

Extensive overcast cloud is caused by generally rising air such as might be forced upwards in a centre of low pressure due to surface inflow. Separate detached cloud may be formed by air caused to rise by being locally heated in contact with a surface having irregularities of temperature. Air may be forced upwards due to wind encountering mountainous land. Cloud so formed is called *orographic*. Wind blowing onshore from the sea often produces cloud over the land while the sky at sea is clear.

Air may also be cooled by contact with a cold surface or at a boundary or front where it meets a colder air mass. When air is cooled below its dew point by contact with the ground, the first effect is that condensation causes water drops to be deposited as dew. If the cooling is sufficient to be conducted upwards ground fog will form which, with continued conduction may grow to some height. In colder conditions when the condensation takes place below freezing point, small ice particles are deposited as hoar frost. Above ground level, warm air in contact with cold air may cause cloud lying along the boundary. Low cloud may reach ground level resulting in mist.

Clouds

The great variety of possible cloud formations are classified in ten main types. These are derived from three basic descriptions which are:

Stratus – cloud that spreads out horizontally and lies in a level layer.

Cumulus – cloud that builds up into rounded heaped forms.

Cirrus – thin fibrous cloud high in the sky

Cirrus is the highest type of cloud. The prefix *cirro* is used to describe high cloud, generally above about five kilometres or 16,404 feet. The lowest cloud is generally below about two kilometres or 6,562 feet. Between and overlapping these heights is medium cloud which is given the prefix *alto*. Another term used is *nimbus* which refers to dark rain-bearing cloud. Generally these clouds are lower in polar regions and higher in tropical regions.

These terms are used to name the ten classes as follows:

High clouds
These are cirroform clouds composed of ice particles above five kilometres (16,404ft) but may be much lower in polar regions. In temperate latitudes they may be up to 13 kilometres (42,650ft) high rising to 18 kilometres (59,055ft) in tropical regions. They are:

Cirrus (Ci)
White and fibrous cloud which may be seen as small detached tufts with hair-like trailing tails or it may lie in bands.

Cirrostratus (Cs)
This is formed when the cirrus thickens and merges to cover the sky in a thin whitish veil which usually produces a halo around the sun or moon. This cloud is usually due to the rising air over a warm front of an approaching depression and as it lowers and thickens is a sign of rain.

Cirrocumulus (Cc)

Formed when cirrus develops into small rounded shapes which may group together in patches or may spread into rippled wave-like areas. The same effect may be produced by the break up of cirrostratus, in which event it will not normally develop into a continuous rain cloud.

Middle clouds

These are at a height above two kilometres and may be up to seven kilometres (22,966ft), again higher at the equator and lower in the polar regions. They may thus penetrate the high cloud region but nevertheless are middle cloud type. They are:

Altostratus (As)

Usually a further development from cirrostratus as the warm air at the front of a depression approaches at a lower height. The sky is mainly overcast with a veil of grey cloud thicker than cirrostratus but through which the sun might be seen as a dimmed grey disk. The cloud may be composed of melting ice particles giving a watery appearance. Some rain or snow may fall but generally the cloud is high enough to allow this to evaporate before reaching the ground.

Altocumulus (Ac)

This consists of white or grey rounded masses or rolls of cloud which may be separated or more usually merged in groups or waves. The rounded form is caused by vertical rising and descending currents in a limited layer, the instability of which prevents the cloud from lying in stratified form. The instability may continue to develop to build up to a heavy shower cloud and possibly thunderstorms. In other conditions, notably in summer, they may simply disperse.

Low Clouds

These exist or have their bases below two kilometres. They are:

Stratus (St)

Low cloud which may form just high enough off the ground to be differentiated from mist or fog. It may envelop higher ground appearing as mist. Its maximum height is about 1,500 feet (500m). It is formed when moist air flows over colder ground or when air rises over higher ground to form mist over the hills. It is generally in the form of a grey mass which may give drizzle.

Stratocumulus (Sc)

This consists of low rounded masses of grey cloud resembling altocumulus but lower and heavier. It is formed when condensation takes place between levels of warm and colder air. It may form waves or rolls covering most of the sky but with patches of light between. It is not generally associated with rain and in winter anticyclonic conditions it can give dull dry weather for long periods. In such conditions the cloud persists due to dust and smoke particles augmenting the condensed vapour.

Nimbostratus (Ns)

This is a dark ragged cloud layer covering the sky and from which continuous rain falls. It is usually the final stage of descending stratus type cloud as a depression approaches. The cloud and rain persist until a clear patch in the sky is the first sign of it breaking up in the instability behind a cold front.

Cumulus (Cu)

These are detached clouds with flat bases and well defined rounded form. The sunlit parts are brilliant white with dark shadow patches. They are formed by rising air which has been heated at ground level. On rising it is cooled and at its dew point condensation takes place forming the base of the cloud. The air will continue to rise building up the cloud until it is cooled to the surrounding temperature. At the same time the rising air sets up downdraughts causing a circulating effect and producing the rounded cloud form. Generally these clouds are detached in a clear sky. They are more common over land which is more irregularly heated than the sea. The heating of the land causes clouds to build up during the day and they tend to disperse with cooling at night. Cumulus may also form over mountains with the base on the windward side as the air is forced up and over the summits. As already mentioned, this is given the particular description of oreographic.

Cumulonimbus (Cb)

This cloud is caused by the continuous build up of cumulus. In a very cold air mass the adiabatic cooling of the rising air may not be enough to overtake the lapse rate of the air mass and the cloud will continue to develop vertically. In such a case the cloud will grow right up through the middle and upper cloud levels and will eventually fragment into cirroform cloud at the top. The vertical development may extend right up to the tropopause where it will spread out into a large flat top. The great vertical depth results in violent updraughts and downdraughts with vertical circulation producing violent squalls at ground level. Rainfall is heavy. The vertical movement within the cloud, up and down through the freezing level keeps the water drops in suspension allowing them to grow, freezing and then melting until they are far too heavy for the cloud and fall as heavy rain or hail showers. The vertical and circulating motion within the cloud also sets up separation and build up of electrical charge resulting in discharge within the cloud and between the cloud and the ground producing lightning and thunderstorm conditions.

Precipitation

Precipitation may be in the form of drizzle, rain, snow, sleet or hail and may be prolonged in continuous fall or pass in showers. In all cases visibility will be affected and may be seriously impaired. Precipitation may be defined as water falling towards the ground in liquid drops or as frozen particles. Sometimes it may not reach the ground but evaporate as it falls when it can be seen as streams of condensation from the base of the cloud.

The ice particles or water droplets of which the cloud is formed are not of sufficient size or density to fall as precipitation. They are suspended in the cloud by circulating currents of air or, if they emerge below the cloud base they evaporate. In order to fall they must grow until they are heavy enough to escape the support of the cloud and fall under the force of gravity as well as being large enough to survive evaporation on the way down.

The very small water droplets formed by condensing vapour will not become ice particles until cooled well below the normal freezing point of water. When ice particles are present however, these supercooled droplets will quickly freeze on the ice particles forming crystals which grow and fall through the cloud. As they fall they usually melt into raindrops and fall as rain. If the temperature is low enough so that they do not melt, but simply join together they form snowflakes and fall as snow or, if melting occurs later, as sleet. Clouds of great depth contain large quantities of water and have vigorous updraughts. The ice particle nuclei then take on coatings of ice as they move vertically within the cloud until they fall.

Small raindrops can however be produced in clouds which are at a temperature above freezing point. They grow by collision and coalescence between the cloud droplets and fall as light rain or drizzle. This accounts for the precipitation which comes from low cloud, mainly drizzle from stratus cloud. The cloud is formed when warm moist air blows over cold lower levels. It has no great depth because the inversion of temperature lapse rate causes the air to be heated with height and produces a flat top to the cloud at the level where it evaporates. There is therefore no tendency for vertical development and large raindrops cannot be formed. By coalescence the condensation grows just enough to fall slowly in dense closely spaced fine drops as drizzle. Drizzle is also caused when moist air is forced upwards over hilly country which may then become enveloped in stratus cloud. This will be confined to land and coastal regions and may obscure landmarks blocking them from view from seaward.

Rain which is continuous and widespread is associated with nimbostratus cloud. This is found at fronts between warm and cold air and within depressions. In advance of a developing depression, the boundary between warm and cold air slopes up with a shallow gradient. As it advances with the cold air in front and below and the warm air behind and above, a sequence of cloud is formed along the front.

This begins with cirrostratus which gradually gets lower and thicker to become altostratus. Rain might begin to fall from this middle cloud and this gets heavier as the cloud continues to lower and thicken to become nimbostratus. The cloud then has great vertical depth and a ragged base from which the rain is persistent. In some cases the warm air may be quite dry and much less cloud is formed. In such circumstances there may be only some low stratocumulus and little or no rainfall.

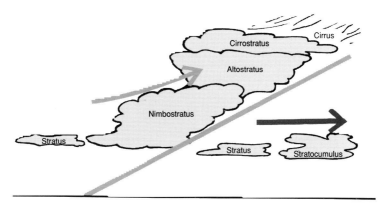

Warm Front

Fig 37

At the cold front the cold air advances behind the warm air. The boundary has a steeper gradient than the warm front. Cloud is altocumulus or altostratus and nimbostratus with cumulonimbus or heavy cumulus. Rain ceases much more abruptly than its onset at the warm front and is followed by showers. This is due to the steeper gradient of the front and the more vertically aligned cloud which allows the sky to clear and remain clear between the cumulus cloud following the front.

Figures (Nos 37 & 38) illustrating cloud at warm and cold fronts are drawn at different horizontal and vertical scales to represent a horizontal length of 300 miles (500km) or more and a height of about 20,000 feet (7km) respectively.

Frontal rainfall varies greatly according to season and to the characteristics of the air mass. Most rainfall is associated with a frontal depression in which case the sequence of warm front and cold front cloud and rainfall follow one another on the equatorial side of the depression. Between the two fronts there is usually stratus type cloud and poor visibility. The warm air is lifted from the surface as the two fronts come together to form an occluded front. The two cloud and rainfall sequences then merge. Along the front rainfall becomes more widespread near the centre of low pressure and can be most extensive over a large area in advance and on the polar side of the centre.

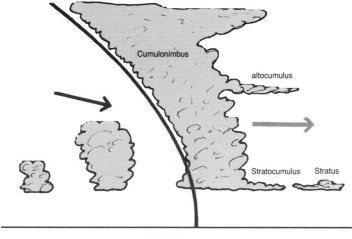

Cold Front

Fig 38

Showers are associated with cumulus cloud. The clouds form in unstable air, particularly in the cold air behind a cold front, and when over the sea there is a plentiful supply of water vapour to be carried aloft by the rising air. Condensation within the cloud can build up large quantities of water where there is deep vertical development and this will result in heavy showers. As the cloud grows it develops from cumulus to cumulonimbus. Ice particles are formed at the upper levels. These provide nuclei upon which further freezing takes place, building up large particles and hailstones. The strong vertical activity holds these in suspension as they continue to grow until they fall from the cloud. As they fall they melt to produce heavy rain, otherwise they reach the ground as hail. As the water content falls out, the cloud will decay, the heaviest rain having fallen first – followed by a gradual slackening and reduction in the size of the drops. In these showers visibility can be seriously affected.

Heavy rain falling from deep cumulus cloud is almost always accompanied by sudden change of wind and squalls which can often be fierce. The surface inflow and rising air is opposed by a downflow of cold air carried down with the heavy rain. This spreads out on the surface below the cloud. There is some evapo-

Cumulonimbus

Fig 39

ration of the rain as it falls below the cloud. Evaporation uses heat which it takes from the air which adds to the fall in temperature between the surroundings and the surface area in the vicinity of the cloud. The result is a sudden onslaught of cold air accompanied by heavy rain. As the cloud passes there are changes of wind and gusts because while the air is being driven down there may still be areas of updraughts.

The development of heavy shower cloud also often produces thunderstorms. The vertical exchange within the cloud causes the water drops to rise and fall and to grow and break up. All matter carries positive and negative electrical charges and the breaking up of the water drops separates these charges. In theory, positive charge tends to be carried up in the updraughts of air in the cloud while negative charge falls with the water drops. In any case there is a separation of opposing electrical charges which accumulation results in discharge between the negative and positive areas within the cloud and between the cloud and the earth. This is seen as lightning and at the same time the sudden expansion, then collapse of air sets up sound waves of compression and expansion which are heard as thunder. Thunder clouds can be isolated or may be in a

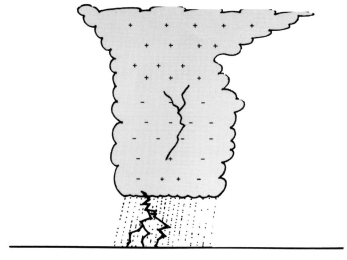

Thunder Cloud

Fig 40

long line of thick squall cloud along a cold front. Lightning, very heavy rain, fierce squalls of wind and severely restricted visibility are features of such a line which can extend for many miles.

It is well known that a flash of lightning can be seen some time before its thunder is heard and that the time between the two is a measure of distance from the storm. At such distance light can be assumed to be received instantaneously while sound takes almost five seconds to travel one mile in air. It follows that the time in seconds between the flash seen and the thunder heard, divided by five, will give you the approximate distance in miles.

Fog

The fog most commonly encountered at sea is caused by warm moist air moving over cold water that is at a temperature below the dew point of the air. The lower levels of the air are cooled upon contact with the surface and condensation takes place. The wind spreads and circulates the fog and the cooling to higher levels. It can be encountered to some depth. The process is known as *advection*.

Advection fog is common when warm maritime air flows from tropical regions to higher latitudes. A good example is the fog of the Grand Banks off Newfoundland. The warm southerly wind arising from the circulation around the sub-tropical high flows northwards in the western North Atlantic and meets the cold water of the drift from Labrador and the Arctic somewhere south of Newfoundland. Hence the dense fog in that region. Generally when the wind becomes strong enough it lifts the fog and some-times leaves only low cloud. In the Newfoundland region however, the difference in temperature between air and sea and the moisture content of the air coming from the Gulf Stream is so great that the fog persists even in a southerly gale, which simply brings in more moist air to feed the fog. With icebergs in the vicinity the area can be one of the most hazardous for the mariner.

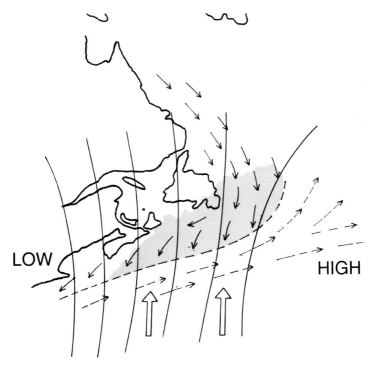

Fig 41

West and south winds of tropical source approaching the colder waters of northern Europe can also produce advection fog. In the same area continental air is heated in summer and approaching from east or south-east can pick up enough moisture from the North Sea or English Channel to produce fog capable of enveloping the coast.

Fog is also found at sea where cold air passes over comparitively warm water. When very cold polar air lies over a warm sea surface, evaporation from the surface immediately condenses and can be seen as swirls of fog. This type of fog is sometimes known as sea smoke. It may become quite dense at low-level but usually evaporates in the drier air above.

Fog forms over land which has been heated during the day and in clear weather loses its heat by radiation when the sun goes down. The air above is cooled, first in contact with the ground where it deposits dew, and then if the cooling is great enough, the condensation grows upwards. This is radiation fog which does not occur over the water because the daytime heat is dispersed in the water and there is much less radiation from its surface at night than on land. Fog from the land may drift over the sea, especially where it flows from hillsides and valleys, being comparatively cold and heavy, and then obscure the coast. Radiation fog can be augmented by smoke and impurities in the air causing it to become dense in industrial areas, affecting rivers and the approaches to ports and harbours. A moderate wind will usually disperse radiation fog but a light wind can induce just enough turbulence in the air above the ground to raise the fog to some height. The ground can sometimes remain dry and the fog appears above ground level.

Mist is the name given to the suspension in the air of minute water drops that reduce visibility but are less dense than fog. Generally mist is simply low cloud lying over hills and land. Mist can lie at sea-level as at a warm front and in the warm sector of a depression, where the surface air is warm and moist and there is cooling from above. The depression of the wet bulb of the hygrometer is good warning of conditions which will allow the formation of fog and mist. When the wet bulb approaches the dry bulb or air temperature, there is little evaporation and the air is near saturation. Any further cooling will cause condensation and the formation of water droplets in the air.

Ice Accretion

If the air temperature is below freezing point, the sea smoke arising from warmer water will freeze into particles of frost. They will remain supercooled until freezing on nuclei and will then immediately form a freezing layer on the hull, superstructure and rigging of any vessel in the vicinity. On fishing vessels in northern waters this is known as black frost.

Freezing spray is another dangerous form of icing. In high latitudes in heavy weather, spray will freeze on the deck, masts and rigging and as it builds up there is more available surface and the deposit is accelerated. The accretion can build up to accumulate top weight enough to render the vessel unstable. Fishing vessels in these circumstances have made for shelter and then when anchored in high wind, driving rain has accumulated the upper ice to such an extent that the vessel has capsized. There is of course the remedy of chipping away the ice, but when aloft in the rigging at sea, this is a difficult and dangerous task. The only sensible remedy is to head for a less cold area.

CHAPTER 3

Waves

Progressive Waves

It is a matter of general observation that a disturbance in smooth water will generate waves which travel along the surface of the water and continue their movement after the cause of the disturbance has ceased. These are known as progressive waves.

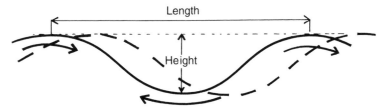

Fig 42

The horizontal distance between two successive wave crests is the *length of the wave*. The vertical distance between the level of crest and trough is the *height of the wave*. The height of the wave is the maximum *amplitude* of vertical movement of any point on the wave.

If the wave is travelling in direction left to right in Figure 42, then after an interval of time the crests and troughs will have moved forward to a new position as shown. It is only the wave form that moves in this way and not the water itself. The movement is much the same as that of a slack rope which is given a shake that will cause undulations to travel along the rope – no part of which has any forward movement.

Obviously however, in the case of waves in water the change from crest to trough and vice versa means that there is a transfer of a volume of water and consequently there must be a movement of water particles. This movement results in a surface flow at the crests in the direction of the progression and in the troughs in the opposite direction.

Ocean Waves

Wind blowing over the surface of the sea generates waves. Friction between the moving air and the water causes the surface water to move with the wind. This movement is imparted to sub-surface layers causing them to move in the same direction but more slowly. The wave motion is therefore set up. As soon as the waves are formed, the force of the wind is applied to the trailing or windward slope of the wave, while the leading slope is to leeward. This imparts further propelling power to the wave, pushing it forward and raising the crests until they break – producing white horses. In strong winds as the waves increase in height, wind eddies may be formed in the troughs in front of the leading wave slope and these increase the breaking effect.

As the wind continues to blow over the sea surface, a continuing supply of energy is supplied to the waves causing them to grow and their velocity to increase. As their speed is increased the waves grow proportionately larger. If the speed is doubled the wavelength will be increased fourfold. The eventual speed and length of the wave will depend on the uninterrupted sea distance over which the wind is blowing in the same direction. This is known as the *fetch* and with sufficient sea fetch the waves may reach a velocity only slightly less than that of the generating wind.

Wavelength Metres	Speed Knots	Period in Seconds
7	6	2
27	12	4
61	18	6
108	25	8
170	31	10
240	37	12
330	43	14
430	49	16

In the open ocean therefore, there is a general relationship between the speed of the wave and its length. The table above gives an approximate relation between waves of different lengths and their speed and period. The period of a wave is the time in seconds for the passage of one complete wavelength over a stationary point. The period is therefore the length of the wave divided by its speed.

The longer wavelengths can only be attained if there is a great enough fetch of wind of sufficient force. For example in the Atlantic Ocean where the fetch may be 1,000 miles, waves of up to 200 metres in length might be expected with gale or storm force winds, while in the Pacific and Southern Oceans, where the wind can blow at strength over greater distances, waves of more than 300 metres in length are experienced.

The relation between the height of the wave and its length is less well defined. Waves can lose their height very quickly while continuing with little change in velocity and length. Generally a wave height of any more than about one tenth of its length cannot be supported without breaking.

When a fresh wind gets up, the waves may reach their maximum height for their length quite quickly and then go on to increase in length and height. Under these conditions there is a general relation between the height of the waves and the velocity of the wind generating them. The following table gives an approximate relation between wind speed (Beaufort Scale and Knots) and the height of the waves that might be expected. The figures tabulated are approximate and may vary in differing circumstances.

Beaufort Scale Number	Mean Wind Speed in Knots	Average Wave Height in Metres
1	2	0
2	5	0.2
3	9	0.7
4	13	1.2
5	18	2.0
6	24	3.0
7	30	4.2
8	37	5.8
9	44	7.5
10	52	9.5
11	60	12.0
12	64 and over	14.5

Waves in deep water are generally steeper over the crests than in the reversed curve of the troughs. The wave form is known as *trochoidal.* A trochoidal curve can be shown by a line traced out by a point within a circle as the circle is made to roll along a straight line. This is illustrated in Figure 43.

The circle has a point 'P' somewhere inside it and is made to roll along the upper straight line from left to right. Point 'P' traces out the shape of a trochoidal wave.

If 'P' is near the circumference of the circle, the wave traced has markedly peaked crests and resembles a wave which has reached its maximum height. This is shown in Figure 43a.

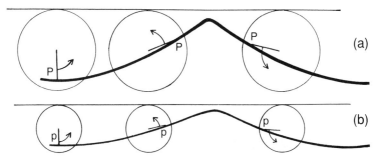

Fig 43

If 'P' is near the centre of the circle, the wave traced has crests which are curved very nearly equally with the troughs and resembles a wave of small amplitude. This is shown in Figure 43b.

Although of different heights the speed of both waves is the same as the speed of the rolling circle. This may be illustrated by imagining the circle turning in a fixed position and the line of the wave moving from right to left.

The speed and direction of movement of the point 'P' relative to the wave represents the movement of the water on the surface of the wave. It is seen to move in the troughs in the opposite direction to the progression of the wave, slowing as it rises up the advancing slope, then changing direction to move forward with the wave as it rises over the crest and then reversing direction again to move backwards into the next trough. Every part of the wave has this motion and this is why something floating on the surface moves to and fro and does not make headway with the wave. The wave does not therefore move forward as a mass but there is to and fro movement of its particles. It is the movement of these particles that gives the wave its force, as for example when it crashes on to rocks and the forward and backward flow of waves running on to a beach.

Below the surface, the water follows the same motion at smaller amplitudes and could be represented by corresponding movement of such points as 'P' in ever decreasing circles as the depth increases. As the height of the wave is increased the velocity of the particles is also increased. This is equivalent to increasing the distance of 'P' from the centre. The peaks of the waves become sharper and at a limiting velocity the surface water at the peaks will break away to be projected forward and fall down the advancing slope. This is when waves break at the crests.

Ocean waves having been generated by the wind will continue for a long time after the wind has dropped. Also waves which have been generated by winds in one area can travel for very long distances away from that area. Waves that have travelled away from the wind that has generated them and waves that continue after the wind has dropped, progress in long rolling motion observed as *swell*. Very rarely or never in the ocean can there be complete absence of swell which in the final stages may be in the form of long waves only a few centimetres high.

Rarely at sea therefore, are waves initiated from a flat surface. Usually they are set up on a sea surface which is already in wave motion. In the commonly experienced circulatory wind systems, changes in wind direction can occur in a short time, as in the passage of a front in a depression. Although the new direction of the wind will have a damping effect, the previous wave motion will continue and the waves experienced will be composed of those set up in the new wind direction imposed upon the earlier ones. This results in waves travelling in different directions causing a confused sea until the new period and wavelength overcomes the old one.

Often the change in wind direction is such that the new waves come from the same general quarter. The two wave motions can then set up a periodic resultant grouping and so generating maximum and minimum group amplitudes. The waves then experienced are composed of those set up by the existing wind added to the old waves and will be the result of the two wave motions of differing periods and lengths.

Fig 44

In Figure 44 a recently generated wave is added to an old wave, producing the resultant wave which consists of groups of high waves where the crests and troughs of the other two augment one another and comparatively low waves between these where the crests and troughs oppose one another.

When two wave motions of some difference in length are travelling in the same direction, pronounced groups of high waves can be set up. These maximum waves will travel forward with a speed of about half that of the constituent waves and will consequently appear to fall backwards relative to the progression of the wave.

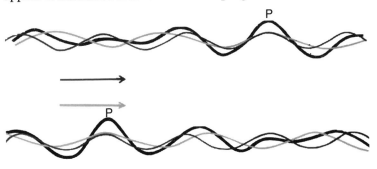

Fig 45

In Figure 45 one constituent wave is longer than the other and is therefore travelling at greater speed. The movement is from left to right. In the upper Figure the crests coincide at 'P' at which point the resultant wave is at its maximum height. In the lower Figure the faster wave has moved on relative to the slower one. The point 'P' at which the waves coincide has moved back relative to the progression.

In this way the highest wave groups appear to travel backwards through the forward wave motion. Where there is little difference in the wavelengths the maximum waves will fall back at about half the speed of the waves.

Tidal Waves

Very long waves are sometimes caused by tremors on the sea-bed. These are often named tidal waves although they have nothing to do with tides. When such a disturbance takes place, the shock causes waves to spread out in all directions. These can travel very long distances and may be experienced on a distant shore as a rise in water level.

Waves having somewhat similar characteristics may be set up by weather conditions. An area of low pressure allows the surface of the sea to rise. The average atmospheric pressure is a little more than 1,000 millibars. That is nearly one ton per square foot or ten tonnes per square metre. A fall in atmospheric pressure to 950 millibars would reduce the pressure on the surface of the sea by about 100lb per square foot or half a tonne per square metre. Such a change in pressure over a wide area would allow a rise in sea-level which would follow the movement of the centre of low pressure and cause a progressive wave motion. A free wave at sea has a natural speed of travel depending upon its length. The wave set up by the depression would in most circumstances have little effect but if the centre is travelling at a speed near the natural speed of the wave there could be a build up into a long wave of significant height.

The circulating winds associated with a deep depression generate waves arising from its centre. In an advancing depression the effect is to produce a tidal type of rising gradient of sea surface ahead of the depression. The long wave so set up has a free movement of its own depending upon its dimensions, and in circumstances where the advance of the depression is in keeping with the advance of the wave there can be a significant rise in the sea surface. The effect is more pronounced in shallower water and if there is coincidence with a high tide there can be quite an extraordinary rise. This is usually associated with a deep depression and the very high tide is accompanied by high winds and storm conditions. The tide comes in the form of a *storm surge*, often causing flooding and damage.

The depth and size of the North Sea make it a vulnerable area for such tidal wave effect when there is a combination of these conditions. There is frequent flooding along the east coast of England and the coast of the Netherlands which from time to time has had devastating effects. The Thames Estuary is particularly affected and this is the reason for the construction of the Thames Flood Barrier.

Waves in Shallow Water

In shallow water the circulation of the wave particles, causing forward movement in the crests and backward movement in the troughs, can extend to the sea-bed and restrict the movement. There is less room for vertical movement and the water simply moves forwards and backwards horizontally as the crests and troughs pass. The depths at the troughs is less than at the crests but since there is no bodily forward movement of water in waves, the volume of water moving back under the troughs must equal the volume moved forward at the crests.

At some point the restriction at the trough retards the circulation so that there is insufficient volume to maintain the wave at the crest. The wave loses its shape, the leading edge steepens and finally the crest breaks.

Fig 46

Arriving at a shelving beach the trough becomes so shallow that very little water can flow back. The volume of water of the oncoming crest can only continue forward and throw itself on the beach in a mass of broken water which is then dragged back at an accelerated rate into the next advancing wave crest.

When waves travel in water which is flowing as a current or tidal stream, the to and fro motion of the waves will take place within the whole body of water which is itself moving with the stream. The two motions are added. Waves progressing with the flow will have an added speed over the ground while waves travelling against the flow will be slowed. In shallow water, such as over a bank, the stream will be speeded up because of the restriction in depth. Waves advancing against the flow in these circumstances could be slowed enough to come to a standstill when they would be seen as a group of *standing waves*. Standing waves may be met at the entrance to an estuary or river channel where they meet an ebb tide. With a strong wind propagating the waves into the entrance against the ebb, they can become steep with continually breaking crests.

Waves Offshore

While a moving body of water such as a tidal stream speeds up in shallows simply because the same volume of water has to pass through a restricted layer, a progressive wave is slowed in shallower water because of the restriction to its circulation. When offshore waves arrive in shallower water they close up and become shorter and steeper than waves in deeper water offshore.

The period of a wave is the time taken between the passage of two successive wave crests. If the period of a wave remains the same, then to reduce its speed, its length must be reduced. On arrival from the deep water the number of waves in a given time remains the same – that is the period does not change. Since the speed is reduced the wave's length is shortened. It is for this reason that shorter steeper waves are encountered inshore. This depends upon the wavelength and the depth of the water.

Offshore also, the sea often tends to be more rough off a headland and to calm down as the waves approach a bay and in the bay the waves approach a beach head-on even though they are travelling parallel to the shore a little distance off. This is a consequence of the refraction of the waves towards the shore. When advancing parallel to a shelving coast or obliquely towards it, the waves have their inshore ends slowed causing them to swing round and approach the shore head-on. Bending towards the shore also causes the waves to diverge as they enter the bay and to converge around a headland. This causes the rougher steeper sea off the headland and calmer conditions in bays. (Fig 47)

Waves are also reflected from the shore, especially if it is a steep rocky coast. When they meet the shore at an oblique angle they may be reflected to leave the shore at an angle equal to the angle of approach. The result of the reflection is that secondary waves are experienced offshore which cross the primary waves. (Fig 48)

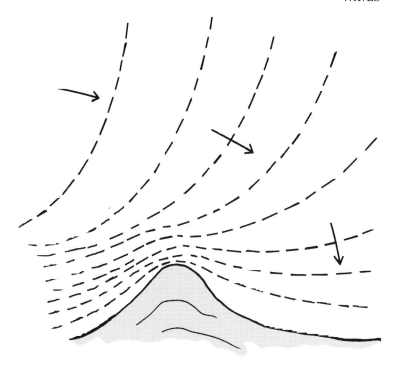

Fig 47

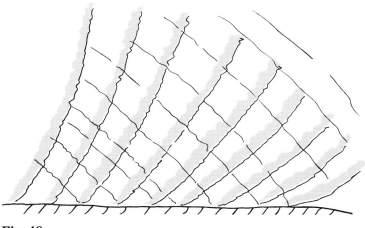

Fig 48

When waves meet the shore head-on their reflection directly back to oppose the primary waves can result in standing waves. These can become quite steep with high crests which shoot up without breaking. On a shelving beach, approaching waves are dissipated without reflection which is a further reason why the sea is sometimes steep and uncomfortable off a rocky or cliff shore, while smoother off a shelving beach.

Standing Waves

Standing waves are formed when waves travelling in one direction meet waves of equal length travelling in the opposite direction. In Figure 49 a primary wave, travelling left to right meets an equal reflected wave, travelling right to left. At position (1) the two waves coincide. The resultant wave is found from the sum of the elevations and depressions above and below the mean line at points along the length of the waves. Since the waves coincide, the resultant wave is in the same position but has double the amplitude of each constituent wave. The points where the wave crosses the mean line (NN) are known as the *nodal points* and are the same for all three waves.

The direction of flow of the water particles in a progressive wave is in the direction of propagation at the crests and in the opposite direction in the troughs. The flow is therefore equal and opposite in each of the constituent waves and the result is no flow at any point in the resultant wave as illustrated at (1)

At (2) the primary and reflected waves have moved forward in their directions of progression. The resultant wave is again found from the elevations and depressions of each. The nodal points of the resultant wave are seen to remain in the same position. At each node the primary and reflected waves are equally disposed above and below the mean line with the result that these points remain the nodes of the standing wave. The direction of flow at the crests and troughs of the primary and reflected waves are shown and seen to result in a flow across the nodes of the resultant wave towards the trough.

At position (3) each wave has progressed through one quarter of a wavelength. Crests and troughs are equally opposed above and below the mean line and the result is flat water. The surface

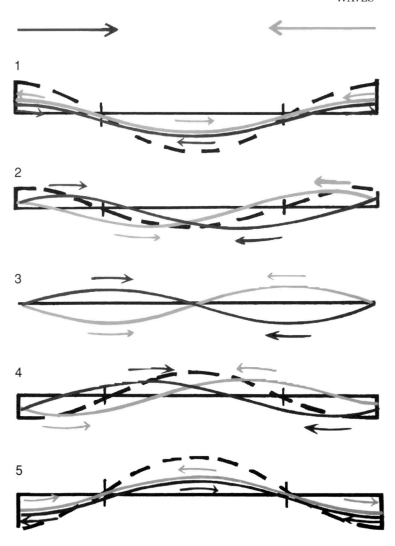

Fig 49

flow of each constituent wave coincides causing maximum flow towards the centre.

At position (4) the waves have progressed further. The nodal points remain in the same positions and the flow is again across the nodes towards the centre.

At position (5) the two waves are again in coincidence and the resultant wave reaches its maximum height. The surface flow of each constituent wave again cancels out and there is no resultant flow.

The wave that results is thus seen to be an oscillation of the water while remaining in the same position. This is known as a standing wave. As the water oscillates the alternating flow from falling water to rising across the nodes is illustrated in Figure 50.

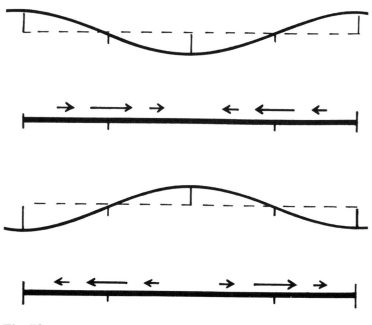

Fig 50

CHAPTER 4

Tides

The main force that generates tide is the gravitational pull of the moon. The force of gravity causes all bodies to be attracted to one another with a force which increases with their mass and reduces with their distance apart. If the mass of a body is doubled, its attraction to another body is doubled. If their distance apart is doubled then the force between them is reduced fourfold.

The earth and moon are attracted to one another by gravity. This allows them to circle one another at the rate of one revolution per lunar day, which is about fifty minutes longer than a solar day. Gravity provides the centripetal force to the centre of revolution, balancing the centrifugal force tending to cause them to fly apart. Because the earth is so much more massive than the moon, the centre of revolution is very near the centre of the earth.

The pull towards the moon applies to the earth itself and also to the waters of its oceans and seas, indeed to all bodies on its surface. Because the force decreases significantly with distance from the moon, the waters on the surface facing the moon experience a greater pull than the waters on the opposite surface which is further away from the moon by the length of the earth's diameter which is about 8,000 miles. The moon is about 240,000 miles away and these dimensions are enough to cause an appreciable angular difference in the direction of pull over the earth's surface.

The moon's gravitational pull therefore differs in force and direction at points all round the earth's surface as shown in Figure 52.

The force shown at the centre of the earth is felt by the earth as a whole and has no apparent effect on a body on its surface including its seas. Force and movement experienced by any body on the

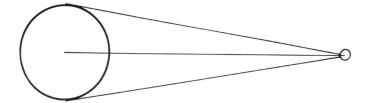

Fig 51

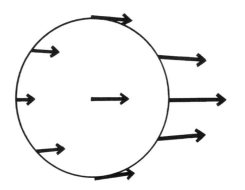

Fig 52

earth is that relative to the earth, that is the difference between the total force applied to the body at its position and the force applied to the earth as a whole. For example, the forces causing the earth to move through space are not felt by those existing on its surface. Our hurtling in a near circle of radius 93 million miles round the sun in a year and circling round the earth's axis at the radius of our latitude every day does not concern us, but we do recognise this when we are propelled at any speed along road or rail. The waters of the earth react similarly to force relative to the earth, which force so applied at any point is the difference between the total force shown in Figure 52 at the place on the surface and the force shown at the centre of the earth.

The force experienced relative to the earth at each point is found by applying the central earth force in the reverse direction and taking the resultant of the two. From a point draw a straight line to represent the central force reversed. From the end of that line draw another to represent the total force at the place.

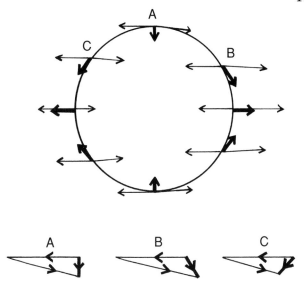

Fig 53

Complete the triangle whose third side represents the relative force which is the tide raising force at any place. The resultant tide raising forces over the earth's surface are in general directed to two points on the surface; one where a line from the earth's centre to the moon would cut the surface and the other diametrically opposed on the side away from the moon. The forces are least around a diameter between these points, where they are vertically downwards, becoming horizontal and increasing, then becoming more vertically disposed upwards towards these points.

The water on the earth's surface is held there by its weight, that is by the force of gravity between the water and the earth. The vertical parts of the tide-generating forces shown, simply increase and diminish that force by an infinitesimally small amount. If we take away the vertical components we are left with horizontal forces as shown in Figure 55. The general effect is, if we imagine the earth to be completely surrounded by water, that the water remains in position with peaks aligned in the directions towards and away from the moon. As the earth rotates daily it carries the surrounding water with it. The surrounding water then, without horizontal bodily movement, keeps its shape with peaks towards and away from the moon.

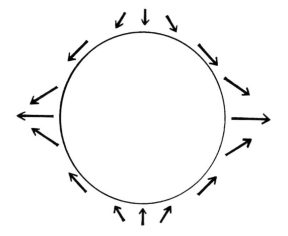

Fig 54

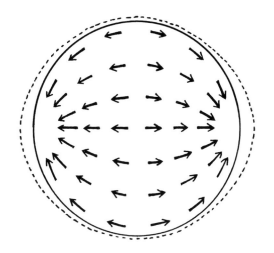

Fig 55

The consequence is that a place on the earth's surface would experience a rise and fall of water, in most places twice daily. Another way of looking at it is that a wavelength equal to half the earth's circumference would continually travel round the earth east to west with a period of half a day.

The daily experience is illustrated in Figure 56. If the moon happens to be in a direction north of the equator then the higher water peaks will be directed north and south in the latitudes shown.

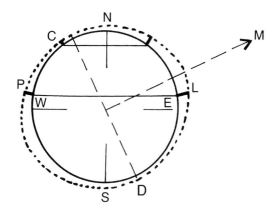

Fig 56

A place on the latitude PL will be carried round by the earth's rotation in the direction west to east. High-water will be experienced at P and the next high-water will be at point L. To an observer on earth the high-waters follow the moon's apparent daily revolution around the earth.

The high-water at L is seen to be higher than the high-water at P. This is a consequence of the moon's direction north of the equator. When the moon is south of the equator in the same circumstances the high-water at P will be greater than that at L. The line between C and D indicates the circle of low-water. It will be seen that in the latitude of C and D there is only one high-water and one low-water in the day. Again, this is the result of the moon's angular distance from the equator – the angle known as *declination*.

We know that the sea does not uniformly surround the earth. Land masses and other forces intervene to produce the actual tides as they are observed. The concept of a uniform sea surrounding the earth in the form of a double wave does however illustrate the obvious features of tides, in that they are experienced twice a day and there is normally an inequality of successive high-waters. It can also be used to illustrate other features such as priming and lagging, springs and neaps and also longer periodic changes.

While the moon is the main influence, the tides do not follow its movement exactly. The sun is very much further away from the earth than the moon but it is also vastly greater in size which causes it to have significant influence on the tides. It is because of the sun's influence that the tides increase and decrease to springs and neaps in about two-week periods.

The moon orbits the earth approximately once a month. When it is on the opposite side of the earth from the sun it is seen fully illuminated by the sun. It is then *full moon* and the moon is said to be in *opposition*.

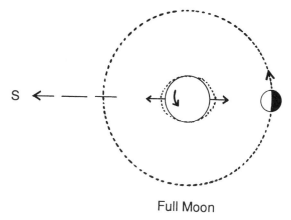

Full Moon

Fig 57

When the moon is between the earth and the sun, the side facing the earth is in darkness. (The illuminated side of the moon is always pointing towards the sun.) It is then *new moon* and the moon is said to be in *conjunction*.

In each case, at conjunction and opposition, the pull of the sun is in alignment with the pull of the moon. The causes the highest high-waters and lowest low-waters giving *spring tides*.

Half way between these positions the direction of the sun is at right-angles to that of the moon. The sun is then pulling in line with the low-water trough, thus raising low-water and consequently lowering high-water. The moon is then said to be in *quadrature*. Obviously there are two positions of quadrature and when the moon is in these positions the height of the high-water is minimum and the height of low-water at its maximum. These are *neap tides*.

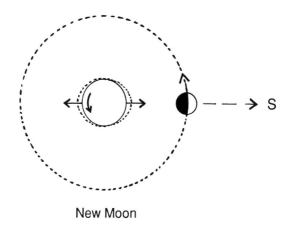

New Moon

Fig 58

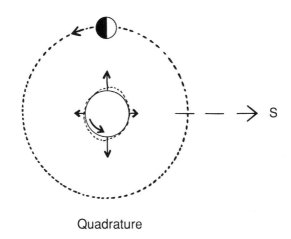

Quadrature

Fig 59

The *range* of the tide is the difference in heights between high-water and low-water. The range is greatest at springs and least at neaps. It will be seen that there are two spring tides and two neap tides in the period during which the moon makes one orbit around the earth relative to the sun. That is the period between one full moon and the next which is a *lunar month*. That is about twenty-nine and a half days.

In Figure 60 the moon is illustrated in its orbit around the earth while the earth orbits the sun – both orbits are anti-clockwise. At position A it is new moon. At position B it is first quadrature, at C it is full moon and at D it is second quadrature. The moon then returns to a position in alignment with the sun, being the next new moon.

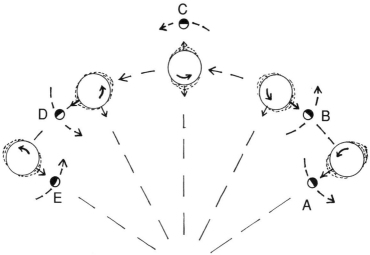

Fig 60

In the interval between successive conjunctions, the earth has moved in its orbit and the moon has to take a little more than one complete revolution round the earth to take up the next position of conjunction. The period to make one revolution of the earth is little more than twenty-seven days, a little more than two days less than the lunar month of twenty-nine and a half days to make a revolution relative to the sun.

At each of these positions high-water occurs at about the time the moon reaches its maximum altitude, that is when it crosses the observer's meridian which is an imaginary line on the earth's surface from the north pole to the south pole through the position of the observer. In the quarters between these two positions of the moon, the gravitational forces to the moon and to the sun are neither in alignment nor at right-angles in direction, but make an acute angle with one another. The resultant force is then inclined a little from the moon towards the direction of the sun.

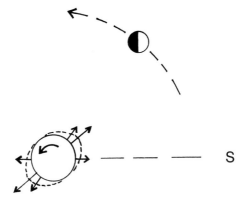

First Quarter — Priming

Fig 61

The position in the first quarter is shown in Figure 61. The direction of the tidal force is a little to the right of the direction of the moon in the Figure. High-water therefore occurs a little before the moon crosses the meridian. The tide is then said to *prime*. The same occurs in the third quarter.

In the second and fourth quarters similar reasoning shows that high-water occurs a little after the moon has crossed the meridian. The tide is then said to *lag*. This is illustrated in Figure 62.

During the first and second quarters, the illuminated part of the moon is growing at which time it is said to *wax*. During the third and fourth quarters the illuminated part is diminishing and the moon is said to *wane*.

There are other variations that cause periodic changes in the tides. For example the moon's orbit is elliptical which introduces a stronger force when it is nearest the earth and weaker when it is at its furthest point. Similarly the earth's orbit around the sun is elliptical, causing the same variation in respect of the sun. The declination of the moon and the sun, that is their distances north and south of the equator, vary. Sometimes they are together in declination and sometimes they are on opposite sides of the equator. All of these variations cause periodic changes, monthly, annually and in periods of five and twenty years.

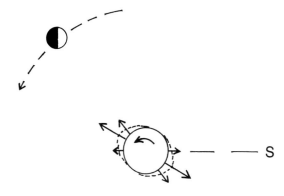

Second Quarter — Lagging

Fig 62

Ocean and Offshore Tides

Continuing the concept of an ocean over the entire surface of the earth. Figure 63 illustrates the direction of the high-water peaks and horizontal tidal forces at a time when the gravitational pull is in a direction inclined to the equator as shown. In the course of a day, a place will be carried round in a complete rotation of the earth. Twelve hours of that movement can be viewed in the Figure as the place moves in the direction west to east.

In that period the changing height of water may be followed by tracing the movement of a position relative to the uniform sea. There is no horizontal movement of the water which maintains its shape and direction in space. The arrows indicate the direction of the horizontal forces maintaining that shape. The water revolves with the earth, simply increasing in depth to the peaks and falling to the troughs.

At A it is high-water. From A to M the level is falling and at M, about three hours after high-water the tide is at its mean level. It continues to fall to C for about another three hours when it is low-water. From C it rises to N when it is again at mean level and about six hours after the low-water the level rises to B, when it is again at high-water. The sequence continues as the position is carried round the other side from B to A. The high-water at A is higher than that at

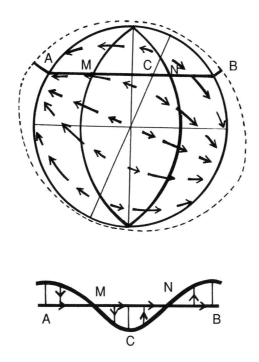

Fig 63

B. Only when the direction of gravitational pull is in line with the equator are the successive high-waters equal at A and B.

The Figure provides a simple explanation of the effect of the tidal force on an ocean freely encircling the earth. But as we know, the waters of the earth form separate oceans and seas and the tides experienced are the result of these periodic forces acting on water which is confined within limits.

The effect of an enclosed area of water of a periodic tidal force directed alternately in one direction and then in the opposite direction is shown in Figure 64.

The force in the direction W to E starts from zero (1), increases to a maximum at (2) before reversing and repeating the sequence from E to W. When the force is acting from W to E the water level is rising at E and falling at W. The maximum difference in height is when the force is zero . The maximum force acts when there is no difference in level. On the return force from E to W the water is rising at W and falling at E.

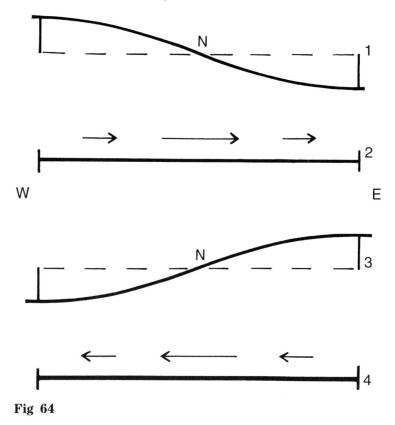

Fig 64

The flow is therefore from falling water to rising water. At mid point there is no rise or fall. That point is the node (N) of the wave form. It will be seen that the form of the wave so produced is the same as that shown in Figures 49 and 50 and is a standing wave. A progressive wave has a maximum flow in the direction of travel at the crest and a flow in the opposite direction in the troughs. The tidal wave form on the other hand has a maximum flow across the noses and is stationary at the crests and troughs. Thus it has a maximum rate at half tide and zero rate at high-water and low-water. The tide may therefore be treated as a standing wave.

The concept might be seen to apply in a restricted channel as in Figure 65. Starting from high-water at W and low-water at E, the flow increases with falling tide at W and rising tide at E and is

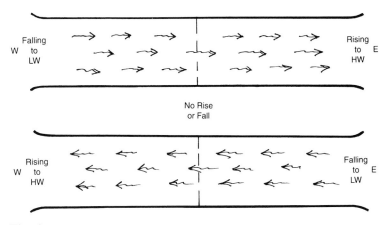

Fig 65

maximum when the levels at W and E are equal. The flow continues, slackening and ceasing when it is high-water at E and low-water at W. The process is then reversed. At mid point there is a nodal line at which there is no rise and fall.

The oceans and seas are large basins and their waters are not restricted as in such a channel. It was shown in Chapter 1 how a flow of air is caused by the earth's rotation to turn to the right in the northern hemisphere and to the left in the southern hemisphere. The same reasoning applies to moving water and this results in a rotating effect on the tidal flow. The result of the rotation on an enclosed expanse of water in the northern hemisphere is followed in Figure 66.

When the flow starts from W towards E, the water begins to fall from high-water at W and to rise from low-water at E. The situation is shown at (a). The effect of the earth's rotation is to cause the flow to turn to the right which causes the water at S to rise and the water at N to fall.

At the time the flow is at its maximum rate the water is level along WE, at which time it has risen to a maximum at S and fallen to a minimum at N. The position is then as shown at (b).

The water continues to rise at E and to fall at W until maximum and minimum levels are reached – during which time it has levelled along NS and the position is shown as at (c).

The flow now reverses and is from E to W causing the water at E

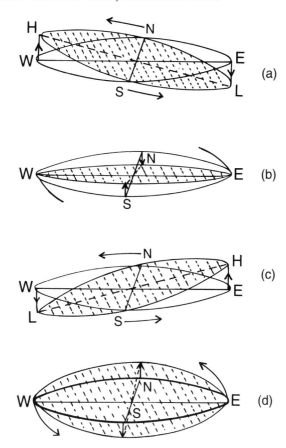

Fig 66

to fall and at W to rise. Again turning to the right, it is caused to rise at N and to fall at S until the position at (d) is reached – following which it continues and arrives back at position (a).

The result is that the tidal motion is not simply to and fro across a nodal line at which there is no rise and fall but a rotating motion with the nodal line rotating anti-clockwise and making one complete revolution in the tidal period. If a line is drawn from the centre of the basin as in Figure 66 to the positions of high-water on the circumference of the basin it will be seen to rotate about the centre in an anti-clockwise direction throughout the twelve hour period. The nodal line of no rise and fall is thus reduced to a single point at the centre. That central point is known as the *amphidromic point*.

In a large open water ocean basin, where the effects of the earth's rotation is significant, instead of the nodal line which resulted in the restricted channel, there is a central amphidromic point of no rise or fall around which the tidal motion is anti-clockwise in the northern hemisphere and clockwise in the southern. If from the amphidromic point lines are drawn through all points at which high-water occurs at the same time, these points will go out like spokes of a wheel and like a wheel will rotate about the central point. These rotating lines are called *cotidal lines*.

Applying this to, for example, the North Atlantic, a tidal diagram should appear somewhat as shown in Figure 67.

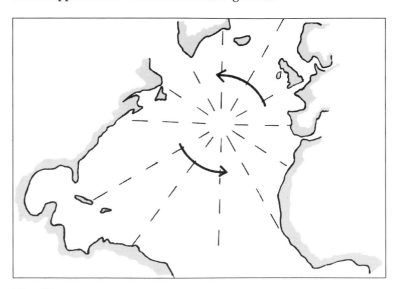

Fig 67

Observation reasonably confirms that the tidal system in the North Atlantic and in oceans generally follow this amphidromic motion. The oceans are not enclosed basins however, their adjacent seas and gulfs have their own circulations which influence the overall tidal motion. In the North Atlantic it appears that the sea north of Scotland and between Iceland and Norway is sufficiently surrounded to set up its own circulation and in the large gulf formed by the east coast of the USA and the north coast of South America there is another circulation. In these circumstances the pattern of cotidal lines for the whole area appears as in Figure 68.

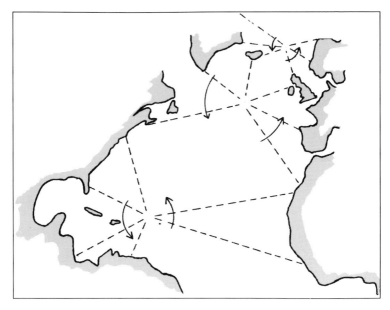

Fig 68

Tides in Gulfs and Channels

We have seen that in an enclosed channel the tidal movement may be expected to follow that of a standing wave such as caused by reflection of a progressive wave as shown in Figure 64. At the closed ends the flow comes to a stop and at mid length the flow is maximum. There is therefore a nodal line at mid length and maximum rise and fall at each end.

If the channel is opened to the ocean outside at one end, water is then free to flow in and out but as before, the flow comes to a stop at the closed end where there is maximum rise and fall. The wave set up in the channel is now no longer constrained by the two closed ends. Its period is of course the tidal period of about

twelve and a half hours and the length, in a channel, of a wave of
that period will depend mainly upon the depth of the channel.

In the simple case where the wave natural to a twelve and a half
hour period is double the length of the channel, the channel
accommodates half a wavelength and the situation is the same as
that in a totally enclosed channel. The range of tide is the same at
the inner end and the entrance. When it is high-water at the outer
end it is low-water at the inner end and vice versa as shown in
Figure 69. There is a nodal line at mid length where inward and
outward flow is maximum and there is no flow at either end.
Obviously therefore there is no actual volume of water entering or
leaving the channel.

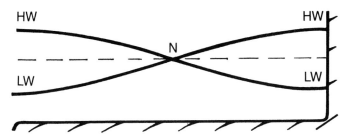

Fig 69

If the length of the channel is a little more than one quarter of its
wavelength, the node would be nearer the entrance and the range
at the inner end would be greater than the range outside as shown
in Figure 70.

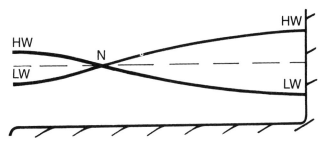

Fig 70

If the length of the channel is less than one quarter of its wavelength there is no node in the channel. High-water and low-water inside are not reversed as before but occur in unison with the tide outside. The water oscillates as if a node existed in the outer ocean and the range in the channel increases along its length from the outer range at the entrance to a maximum at the inner end as in Figure 71.

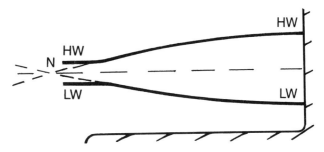

Fig 71

In each of these two cases the water flows inwards across the node, real or virtual, beginning from zero when it is low-water in the channel, increasing to a maximum rate at mid tide then decreasing to high-water. It then reverses and flows out. A volume of water thus enters and leaves the channel and in it the water is caused to oscillate with an amplitude which is greater, the nearer the node is to the entrance. When the node is in the near vicinity of the entrance the amplitude becomes a maximum and there is a great rise and fall at the inner end. This is a condition know as *resonance*, much the same in theory as the resonance in an organ pipe when a sound wave of the resonant frequency is applied.

The natural period of oscillation of water in a channel depends upon its depth. In a channel of about twenty-five fathoms (twelve metres) depth, a wave of period coinciding with the tidal period would have a length of about 500 nautical miles. Its quarter wavelength is therefore about 125 miles. A closed gulf of such depth and length might then be expected to oscillate in near resonance with the tide outside and have a large range at the inner end. A good example of this is the Bay of Funday between Nova Scotia and mainland Canada which, with a depth and length approximating the above, has a range of tide of more than twenty metres. In

British waters the Bristol Channel has similar dimensions and has a range of tide of more than fifteen metres.

A channel of length three quarters of its critical wavelength could also have a node at the entrance. Its oscillation in resonance with the tidal period would then be in the form of a loop with another node one quarter wavelength from the inner end as in Figure 72.

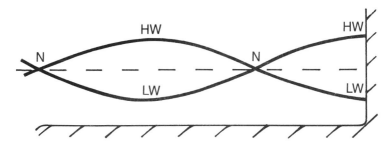

Fig 72

In a channel open at both ends, the tides are responsive to the rise and fall at each end. Where these are nearly in unison the tide will have a maximum rise and fall about mid length and will oscillate somewhat in the form shown in Figure 73.

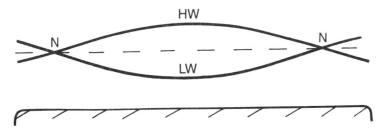

Fig 73

The length of the channel is rather more than half a wavelength and there are nodes near each end. There could be variations of this with one or other node nonexistent in a virtual position outside as in Figure 71 but generally the water would rise and fall over much of the channel with maximum range near mid length. If the length of the channel is very near half wavelength the nodes would be at each end resulting in resonant oscillation and large mid length range of tide. The next resonant length would be one and a half wavelength in which case there would be a node at each end and another in the middle with two points of alternating maximum high and low-water as in Figure 74.

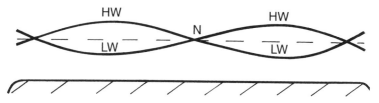

Fig 74

Where there is a significant difference in the tides at each end of the channel, two separate systems may be set up which have to come to terms with one another. This will result in a less symmetrical wave form and a less straightforward distribution of the tidal oscillations.

Tides as Observed

The waters around the British Isles provide useful areas for comparison of theory and practical observation.

There are three substantial enclosed water areas with openings to the ocean around the British Isles in which the observed tide might now be compared with the theoretical explanations of tides in gulfs and channels. These are the Irish Sea, the English Channel and the North Sea.

The Irish Sea

The sea forms a basin between Ireland and the north-west coast of England. Entrance from the ocean through the channel between north-east Ireland and south-west Scotland in the north, and between Ireland and Wales in the south, provides an example of an open-ended tidal area. High-water occurs in both those channels at about the same time. The tides at the open ends are therefore in reasonable unison and we should expect a standing oscillation in the Irish Sea basin as shown in Figure 73.

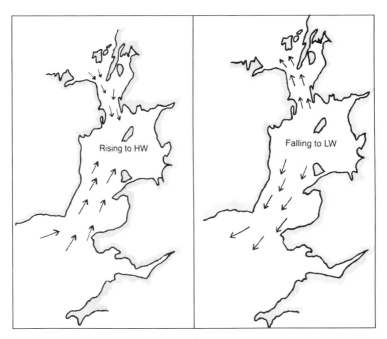

Fig 75

Observation confirms that high-water occurs at about the same time over the whole basin between south-west Scotland and north Wales. According to the theory there should be a nodal line positioned near the northern end between Ireland and Scotland and another across the southern end between Ireland and Wales. This however is on the real rotating earth and according to further theory those nodal lines can be expected to be reduced to amphidromic points.

The times of high-water around the northern channel show that high-water progresses with an anti-clockwise circulation around a centre somewhere in mid-channel. From the south, high-water advances faster up the Welsh coast than on the Irish coast. This is in accordance with the explanation of rotary tides. At the same time the tidal stream under the Coriolis force tends to turn to the right and builds up higher tides on the Welsh coast and the range of tides there is greater than that on the Irish coast.

Fig 76

The English Channel

The tidal movement in the English Channel is much the same and at the same time as that in the Irish Sea. High-water proceeds from the Western Approaches eastwards to about the Isle of Wight at the same time as it travels north from Land's End. At the other end high-water enters from the North Sea through the Dover Strait. Between these points high-water occurs almost simultaneously in standing oscillation.

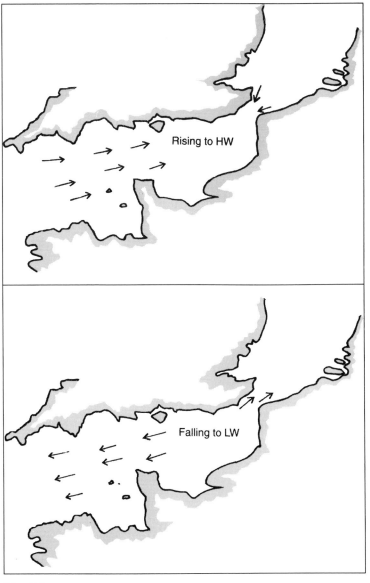

Fig 77

As in the Irish Sea there should be a node near each end. The node at the eastern end is outside in the North Sea, somewhere between south-east England and the Netherlands. High-water progressing around that point in anti-clockwise motion enters into the Dover Strait. At the Western end high-water proceeds along the French coast faster than along the English coast, indicating an anti-clockwise progression with a virtual centre somewhere inland a little west of the Isle of Wight.

As in the Irish Sea, the stream tends to turn right and proceeding up-channel builds up high-water along the French coast while when running down-channel it builds up higher water along the English coast. The result is a greater range of tide along the French coast than that along the south coast of England.

Fig 78

The North Sea

The North Sea is a partially enclosed sea with an opening to the ocean in the north, an opening to the Baltic Sea in the east and a restricted opening at the southern end at the Dover Strait. Its dimensions are consistent with the requirements of tidal oscillations similar to those illustrated in Figure 74, showing two half wave standing oscillations with a node between them and a node at each end.

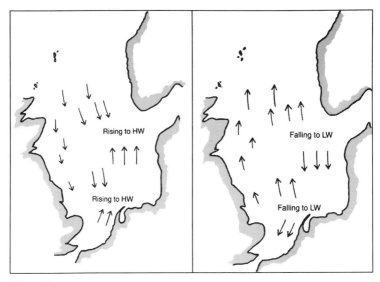

Fig 79

Observation shows the nodes to be reduced to amphidromic points around which high-water circulates anti-clockwise. There is one between Scotland and Norway and another between north-east England and Denmark. Between these there is a standing oscillation. The southern amphidromic point is that which serves the eastern end of the English Channel and between these there is another standing oscillation.

The circulating tide sends the stream southwards down the east coast of Scotland and England and northwards up the eastern side of the North Sea. Over the two areas of standing oscillation high-water takes place at the same time.

The tidal movement in the seas around the British Isles is thus seen to be in reasonable agreement with the described theory of tides in gulfs and channels. Similar comparison may be made in partially enclosed waters elsewhere.

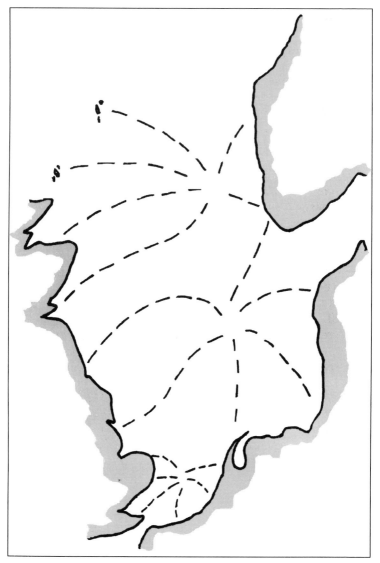

Fig 80

Shallow Water Tides

Earlier in this chapter when dealing with tidal movement in a channel, it was stated that the length of a wave of tidal period depended upon the depth of the channel. The period of a wave is the time for the passage of one wavelength. It follows that the rate of travel of the wave depends upon the depth of the water. It was stated that in a depth of twelve metres a wave of tidal period, about twelve and a half hours, would have a length of about 500 nautical miles. The wave would therefore travel at about forty knots. In a depth of about twenty-four metres the length would double to about one thousand nautical miles and the rate of travel would be about eighty knots. The relationship is a result of the energy of the travelling wave and the volume of water.

The reduction in speed of the wave has no relevant significance in deep water becoming less deep. In shallow water the difference in depth between high and low-water can be considerable, causing the crest to travel faster than the trough. The result is shown in Figure 81.

The crest is advanced and the trough retarded relative to the uniform wave. This results in a steeper slope of advance and a shallower gradient behind the crest, causing the incoming tide to run faster than the outgoing tide. The difference between the tidal wave and the uniform wave is shown by the lower wave in the Figure. If at points along the lower wave, its height – positive above and negative below the mean line – are applied to the uniform wave above, the result is the tidal wave. The lower wave can then be considered to be a shallow water correction to be applied to the uniform tidal wave to obtain the shallow water tidal wave.

The shallow water correction wave is seen to have half a wave-length of the tidal wave. The tidal movement in shallow water can thus be considered as a standing oscillation made up of a primary uniform wave and a secondary wave much the same as described for a primary wave and a reflected wave. In this case the secondary, or correction wave, takes the place of the reflected wave and it is of half the period of the primary.

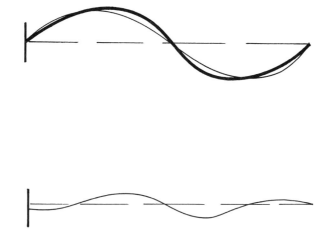

Fig 81

Double Tides

In some places the tide may 'stand' for a prolonged period at high-water or at low-water and in some places, instead of simply standing at high-water, the level will fall then rise again before falling to the next low-water, so producing a double high-water. Similarly, a double low-water might be produced. The usual cause of this is the particular resultant of the primary oscillation and the secondary shallow water correction wave.

The resultant of any two waves having the same period can only be another wave of the same period or no wave if they happen to be equally opposed to one another. This can be seen in Figure 49. Two separate tidal movements such as coming in from two ends of a channel, will have equal periods and will only result in one single high-water and one single low-water or – like the equally disposed waves – no rise or fall. To obtain a double tide it is necessary to have a secondary wave of half the period or less of the primary wave. Depending upon the relative dispositions of these waves, a double high-water or low-water may result.

As we have seen, the resultant of any two waves is found by adding the elevations and depressions above and below the mean level at all parts. In Figure 82 one constituent wave is of half the wavelength of the other. When these are situated relative to one another as shown they combine to produce the resultant wave which is seen to have two high-waters and one low-water.

Fig 82

In the Figure the longer line is the primary wave and the shorter line is the secondary wave. If the secondary wave is moved through half a wavelength relative to the primary wave the result would be a double low-water and a single high-water.

The rise and fall and duration of double tides can be further complicated by other factors. In general however, conditions are favourable for double tides when there is a marked shallow water effect and the range of the primary tide is small enough to allow the secondary shallow water effect to be significant.

The range of tide generally increases with distance from an amphidromic point. Near such a point therefore, the range is not usually great and in shallow water there is the possibility of double tides. In the English Channel we have seen cotidal lines radiate from an area somewhere inland a little west of the Isle of Wight. On that part of the coast from the Solent to Portland there are expanses of shallow water. Conditions are suitable for double tides and these do occur at Southampton, Poole and Portland.

The rise and fall of tide is conveniently depicted by a curve of heights over the tidal period. At a place where there are no disturbing influences the curve may be well defined and fairly uniform as shown in Figure 84 for spring and neap ranges. Between springs and neaps the rise and fall is somewhere between the two.

The curves are not often of such uniform shape. Figure 85 shows the type of curves associated with double high-water. There is distortion of the incoming tide which causes a stand at high-water and at springs a reversal of flow and a secondary rise after the main high-water peak has passed. There is something of a stand at neaps also but not sufficient to produce the double high-water.

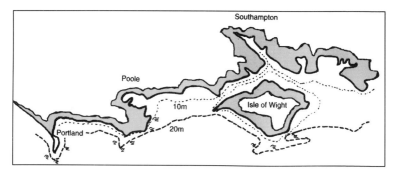

Fig 83

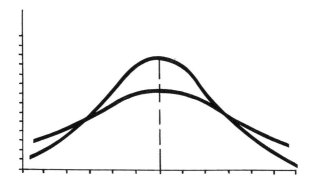

Fig 84

In other circumstances the tide might stand at low-water or suffer a reversal of flow and fall in level after the main low-water has passed, thus producing a double low-water as illustrated in Figure 86.

Tidal Races and River Bores

Tidal overfalls, races and eddies are commonly experienced at places where the tidal stream encounters shallowing water and where it passes through a narrowing channel. Clearly, if a compar-

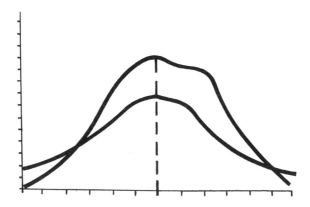

Fig 85

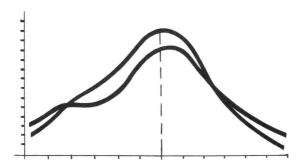

Fig 86

atively deep water tidal stream flows into a narrower channel the rate of flow must increase to allow the volume of water to pass. The same applies to a tidal stream flowing over shallows. The result is a distortion of the surface of the water. The first indication is usually a depression of the water surface with signs of races and eddies. With further restriction the depressions may disappear and the flow build up to produce turbulence and broken water.

Pressure in water increases with depth. Just as altitude can be measured by the difference in pressure from sea-level because of the uniform fall in atmospheric pressure with height, so too can depth be measured by the increase in pressure below sea-level. In fast flowing water, however, pressure below the surface is found to be less than that at the same depth in still water. When a flow of water is speeded up over shallows or at a constriction it therefore suffers a reduction in pressure.

To cause the water to be speeded up a force, that is a pressure, must be applied. The water is accelerated from a higher pressure to a lower pressure. It follows that water speeded through a restriction is under a reduced pressure. When it emerges from a restriction it slows down and so is emerging into a higher pressure.

A result of this reduction in pressure in the water is that at the restriction, it has less resistance to the atmospheric pressure that pushes down on the surface and causes it to be depressed below the normal mean level. Water flowing over a shallow patch caused by a rise in the sea-bed will therefore be depressed at the shallow and where the bed is uneven, the water surface may mirror in reverse the undulation of the bottom as shown in Figure 87. This effect produces turbulence and eddies and if the pressure is sufficiently reduced water rushes into the depression to create whirlpools.

Fig 87

A limit may be reached if the water is flowing too fast, in which case it will build up over the shallow and tumble and break. The surface will then be thrown up over the rises on the bottom and mirror these in the opposite manner to the flow below the critical speed.

Fig 88

Similarly, through a narrow constriction the accelerated water shows a surface depression and turbulence. There is a limit above which increased flow will be built up to breaking point, resulting in tumbling and breaking waves.

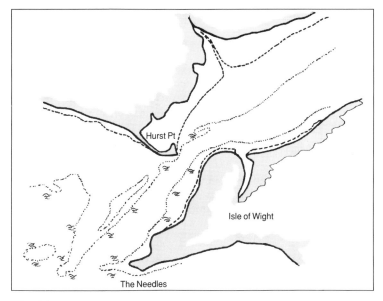

Fig 89

One example of this is the Needles Channel between the western tip of the Isle of Wight and mainland England. The tidal stream flowing between the Solent and the outer waters of the English Channel is restricted through the narrows at Hurst Point. Heavy overfalls are experienced and there are examples of broken water over the shallow Shingles Bank that lies to the west of the channel where the main tidal stream encounters a sudden reduction of depth.

A tidal stream flowing into an estuary or the mouth of a river will generally be flowing into shallowing and probably narrowing water. As the stream flows over the rising bed of the channel, its speed will be increased and the surface will be depressed. In such conditions there is a limiting speed beyond which the stream can no longer flow smoothly and then it will start to build up and break. When the water becomes very shallow the stream may be increased beyond its critical speed and build up into an advancing wave. In this way a tidal bore is formed.

Fig 90

A bore will travel up a river in the form of a well defined wave and maintains higher water behind it. The height of a bore can be several feet. Its speed of advance depends upon the depth of water behind it; the higher the water the faster it travels. This effect, which can be spectacular, is of a wall of water with high running water behind the advancing wave proceeding up river with a wavefront spanning the river from bank to bank.

Depth is usually greater in the middle of a river than at the sides and since the speed of a bore depends upon the depth it would appear that the wave in mid-channel should proceed ahead and dissipate behind the wave and towards the river banks. However, the volume of water is so great that the water is forced over the shallow edges and the bore advances as a straight wave spanning the width of the river.

Tidal bores are most likely to be generated where there is a rising gradient to shallow banks at the mouth of the river. After low-water when the incoming tide is flowing over shallows its rate may become sufficiently strong to set up a bore. This is more likely to happen at spring tides. At neap tides the flow might not be strong enough nor the water low enough for the speed critical at that depth to be exceeded. The bore may therefore only appear for a number of tides before and after springs.

In some cases the bore might not start at the river entrance but somewhere up-river where it becomes shallow or where there are narrow stretches. Bores are most likely to be formed at the mouth of a river where a narrow entrance opens to a shallow estuary. These conditions exist at the River Seine which has a narrow entrance at Le Havre and a wide shallow estuary. The incoming flood tide flows over shallows to the entrance and forms a bore which travels up-river as far as Rouen.

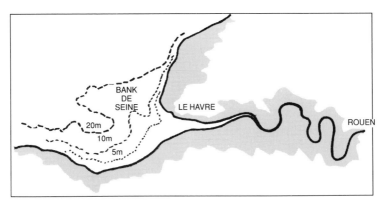

Fig 91

In England there is a bore on the River Severn. The river opens up over shallow banks into the Bristol Channel. The incoming tide from the estuary is speeded up at the narrow and shallow entrance causing the bore to form and travel up-river. There are spectacular bores in other parts of the world, for example on the Tsein Tang River in China which flows into the estuary of the Hangchow Bay.

Ocean Currents

It has been seen that wave motion is generated by wind blowing over the water surface and that the motion is oscillatory resulting in a to and fro movement without any bodily progression. Quite apart from the wave motion, the prevailing winds over the oceans impart a momentum to the water causing a general movement of the surface. Ocean currents are generally caused in this way. There is also bodily movement of water caused by exchange between different temperatures and densities. Such displacement can be vertical as well as horizontal. Currents can also be funnelled through straits and speeded round headlands in the same way that winds are funnelled.

The overall result is a general mass movement of the surface of the oceans following the prevailing wind directions. The movement of the water is affected by the revolution of the earth in the same way as described for winds, turning to the right in northern

115

latitudes and to the left south of the equator. Thus currents closely follow the wind circulation.

The main ocean current circulation is therefore around the areas of sub-tropical high pressure in the northern and southern oceans. The exception is in the Indian Ocean north of the equator, where the currents follow the seasonal monsoon changes. In the Southern Ocean the current has a clear flow from west to east following the prevailing westerly wind.

Figure 92 illustrates the general circulation in the oceans. In the North Atlantic the circulation round the sub-tropical high causes a North Equatorial current to flow westwards. This turns northwards and is accelerated through the islands and into the Gulf of Mexico from which it emerges through the Florida Straits. Travelling up the east coast of the United States as the warm Gulf Stream the flow turns north-east towards the British Isles where it is responsible for the relatively high water temperature for that latitude.

The North Atlantic circulation is completed as the current turns back towards the equator. Some of the flow passes into the Mediterranean where the northern hemisphere tendency to turn to the right sets up an anti-clockwise circulation. Part of the northerly flow flows round the north of Scotland and into the North Sea where again it circulates anti-clockwise. Some of the northern flow is into the Arctic Ocean and westwards towards Greenland. Following the low pressure wind circulation, cold Arctic waters flow southwards on the east coast of Greenland and northwards up its west coast to turn to join the southward Labrador Current, the waters of which meet the Gulf Stream and being much colder and more dense, sink below the warmer water.

There is similar circulation in the Pacific Ocean. The warm stream from north of the equator flows up past the Philippines to Japan. This is the Japan Current or Kuro Shio that corresponds to the Atlantic's Gulf Stream. It travels eastwards to the west coast of North America and then south as the California Current to return to the North Equatorial Current. Cold water flows south from the Bering Sea to meet the warm Kuro Shio and sink as does the Atlantic's Labrador Current. There is an anti-clockwise circulation round the Bering Sea and the same in the Gulf of Alaska.

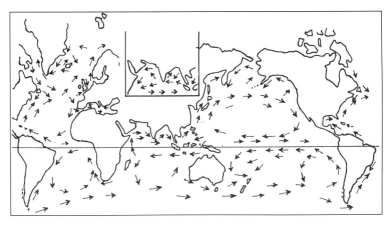

Fig 92

In the Indian Ocean north of the equator and the Bay of Begal and the Arabian Sea, the general drift is eastwards in the summer during the south-west monsoon and north-east in the China Sea to join the Japan Current. In winter during the north-east monsoon the flow is south-west through the China Sea and westwards in the Indian seas with a clockwise circulation set up to the north in the Bay of Bengal.

The southern oceans have anti-clockwise circulations round the sub-tropical highs. These set up west-going streams south of the equator and between these South Equatorial currents and the North equatorial currents in the same direction, there are Counter Equatorial east-going currents. In the Indian Ocean in summer there is no west-going current north of the equator as the flow there is eastwards with the monsoon.

In the southern oceans the west-going currents south of the equator turn south forming the Brazil Current on the east coast of South America, the Mozambique and Aghullas Currents on the east coast of southern Africa and setting up a circulation between the east coast of Australia and New Zealand. On the southern side the drift joins up as the Southern Ocean Current of eastward flow round the Antarctic. On the eastern sides of the oceans, the flow turns northwards as the Peru Current on the west coast of South America and the Benguela Current on the west coast of southern Africa. Rounding Cape Horn some of the east-going flow turns north up the east coast of South America as the Falklands Current, eventually meeting and sinking below the warmer Brazil Current.

The currents generally have a rate of flow in their main stream in the open ocean of from half a knot to two knots. Where the current meets a coastline its rate can be increased and the flow through straits and between islands can be accelerated.

CHAPTER 5

Ships and Boats in Waves

Wake

The sight of circular waves spreading out from a centre of disturbance in calm water is common. If a stone is thrown in for example, water is displaced then falls back into the cavity setting up expanding circles of waves. Similarly, as a vessel moves forward water is displaced then falls back into place as it passes. As the vessel proceeds it generates waves which spread out in circles from centres along its track.

For the most part these waves are absorbed into the surrounding water and disappear. Parts of them however, are travelling at such speed and direction relative to others that they reinforce and form group waves which persist. At a particular distance and direction from the vessel where this critical interaction occurs, group waves are maintained and travel along keeping station with the vessel. These produce the wave form of a vessel's wake.

In Figure 93 a vessel travels from P towards S along the straight-line track shown. As it proceeds waves are generated which travel out in expanding circles from centres along the track. Some of these will form the group waves of the wake. By the time the vessel has arrived at S, one such wave circle from P will have arrived at the position marked M. At the same time waves travelling at the same speed from successive points along P—S will have gone out for proportionately smaller distances and arrived at positions along a straight line from S to M. That line is the wavefront of all the waves travelling in the direction P—M which could constitute the waves of the wake.

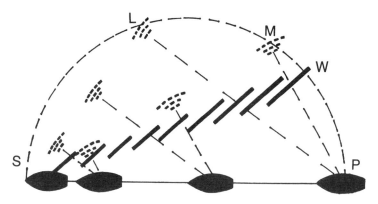

Fig 93

The waves travelling in another direction, P—L for example, form a wavefront along the line S—L. In general, any straight line from S to the semicircle drawn on P—S could form a wavefront of the waves travelling from P. Similarly, wavefronts could be drawn for the position of the vessel at any point between P and S. Of these waves however, only those which reinforce one another to form group waves will form the wake. The remainder are soon dissipated.

We have seen in Figure 45 how the interaction of two wave motions travelling in the same direction and at the same speed, will form group waves which travel forward with a speed of half that of the waves which form them, and that these group waves fall back as the constituent waves proceed. In Figure 93 the group waves which are formed by the interaction of the waves to M and the waves from L will be along a front which is halfway between P and M and also halfway between P and L, since they are travelling at half the speed of the waves that form them. The same applies to the other positions of the vessel shown along P—S and the result is that the wavefront of the group waves is from the position of the vessel at S along the line S to W.

These group waves so set up form a bow wave which extends on each side of the vessel at an angle of about 20° to the fore and aft line. This angle is constant and does not change with a vessel's speed. The bow wave is not a single wave but is made up of short parallel waves which maintain station with the vessel while travelling outwards in a direction of about 35° from the track.

In addition to the bow waves, the pattern of waves set up by a vessel under way includes a series of waves following directly astern. As the vessel moves through the water there is friction between the hull and the water. This slows the flow along the hull and tends to carry a layer of water along with the vessel. This layer of water increases along the length from bow to stern resulting in a quantity of water falling in behind the vessel and being dragged along astern. At the same time there is in addition, an inrush of water to replace that displaced by the vessel as it moves forward. (A propeller thus turns in water which has forward movement.)

The effect of all this activity astern is to cause a general turbulence which generates waves of different wavelengths and which travel out in circles as do all waves caused by a disturbance in the water. By the same reasoning as applied in Figure 93 these wave circles produce group waves from the stern similar to those from the bow.

Stern waves diverge and follow parallel to those from the bow. However the maximum wave-making action immediately astern is directed aft and it is in line astern that waves of critical speed and length are continually generated to form group waves travelling at the same speed as the vessel. The result is a train of waves following directly astern.

We have seen that there is a relationship between the speed of a wave and its length. The waves that follow astern thus have a wavelength corresponding to the vessel's speed. The diverging bow and stern waves are apparently falling back at half the speed of the waves from which they were formed. When their angle of progression relative to the vessel is taken into account, it is found that their wavelength is two-thirds the length of the waves following astern.

These wavelengths apply only in water deep enough to allow the free movement of wave motion. As has been shown, the speed and length of a wave depends upon the depth of water. In water of reduced depth the wave is constrained within a maximum allowed by depth.

To make waves a supply of energy is required. Much of the power used to keep any craft moving forward through the water is

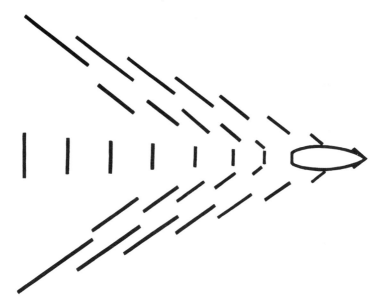

Fig 94

spent in making waves. In shallow water where the wake is constrained, the waves are reduced and less power is needed to maintain the same speed. In shallow water where the waves cannot
keep pace it may be found that speed increases without apparent
reason.

Power is also used in overcoming frictional resistance. That
resistance depends upon the area of contact between the hull and
the water and also upon the nature of the surface of the hull. A
smooth surface allows a smooth laminar flow of the boundary
water layer. A rough surface and projections of any kind set up turbulence in the flow and eddy formation which absorbs more
energy. It follows as is generally obvious that most economical
fuel consumption and best results under sail are obtained with a
clean smooth underwater hull.

In shallow water where there is little under-keel clearance there
is frictional effect between the water which is moving with the
vessel and the sea-bed. (Obviously this does not apply to fin-
keeled yachts which would run aground before the effect
occurred or to planing craft not in displacement mode). This

causes a reduction of the buoyant support, allowing the vessel to sink deeper in the water and thus increasing its draught. This sinkage is known as 'squat' and can be the cause of touching bottom and grounding if excessive speed is used. Where there is little clearance and in a narrow channel, the replacement of water displaced by the hull is retarded. Water builds up at the bow and stern and the waves of the wake being constrained in length become steep and can be destructive. The effect can only be minimised by proceeding at suitably reduced speed.

When moving close to a bank in a channel a lateral effect similar to squat can be experienced. There is a reduction in pressure between the hull and the bank which causes the craft to be attracted towards the bank. Since the majority of vessels are of fuller form aft, the effect is to bring the stern in towards the bank and to cant the bow off. In a curving channel it may be found that the vessel follows the curve to some extent without change to the helm. This is commonly experienced in larger ships in narrow waters and is referred to as a ship 'feeling' the channel as she apparently steers herself round bends. It would be unwise however, to place any reliance on this effect as the stern being pulled into the bank can result in misfortune. It is safer to take the bends slowly and with caution.

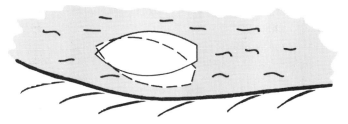

Fig 95

The same principle applies if a quay wall is approached too fast or where two craft pass too closely to one another. The effect has frequently caused damage to large merchant ships. It would be rare to allow two ships under-way to pass in such close proximity, but it is not uncommon to find one ship approaching a berth to pass close to another berthed at the quay. As it passes at apparently slow speed, the docked vessel is affected by the attraction which can be strong enough to part her mooring lines and to bring her bodily out to collide with the passing vessel. (This has given rise to claims that the passing craft did nothing wrong – the other ship simply came out and hit her!) Going alongside a vessel at anchor provokes the effect even more, even to smaller craft.

Stability

Any craft floating in still water is maintained in equilibrium under the equal and opposite forces of its weight – acting vertically downwards – and the buoyancy of the water – acting vertically upwards. The weight acts through the vessel's centre of gravity, the position of which depends upon the distribution of weight on board. The force of buoyancy acts through the centre of buoyancy which is the geometrical centre of the underwater volume.

The centre of buoyancy will be in the fore and aft centre plane. (Unless of some special unsymmetrical design below the water-plane.) For a stationary vessel to float upright in still water therefore, the centre of gravity must be in the same centre plane and in a vertical line with the centre of buoyancy. This requires all weight aboard to be equally distributed on each side of the fore and aft centre line.

Figure 96a illustrates a vessel floating upright. G is the centre of gravity and B the centre of buoyancy. The force acting down through G is equal to the force acting up through B and each is equal to the total weight of the vessel and its contents. That total weight is the vessel's *displacement*, usually denoted by W and may be defined as the weight of water displaced by the vessel as she floats at that particular draught.

If a vessel is heeled by some external force, its centre of gravity will remain in the same position as long as there is no shift of weight on board. The centre of buoyancy will however move to a new position which is the geometrical centre of the displaced volume which is now a different shape. The new position is shown as B' in Figure 96b.

The weight acting vertically downwards and the buoyancy acting vertically upwards are now out of vertical alignment and together they produce a *righting moment* which acts to take the vessel back to its upright position. The magnitude of the righting moment depends upon the displacement (which has not changed)

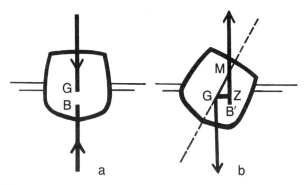

Fig 96

and the distance apart of the lines of action of the two equal forces.

The distance between the lines of action (weight and buoyancy) is shown by the line GZ in Figure 96b. This is the *righting lever*. It is drawn from G at right-angles to the line of action of the force of buoyancy through B'. The righting lever varies with the angle of heel and since the displacement remains constant (with no weight added or removed) comparison of the righting moments at different angles of heel in that condition can be made by comparing the lengths of the righting lever as the heel is increased.

The length of the righting lever at varying angles of heel can be plotted to provide a curve showing the stability of a vessel for its particular loaded condition. Such a curve is shown in Figure 97. The lengths of G—Z are plotted against the angle of heel as shown.

At position 1, at a small angle of heel there is a small righting lever. This indicates a reasonably gentle motion returning the vessel to the upright in an easy manner. A large righting lever at this stage would result in a more violent and jerky motion. As the craft heels further, the righting lever increases reaching a maximum at about position 2.

Clearly when a vessel reaches such an angle a good righting lever is required. As the craft comes upright, the righting lever will diminish which is advantageous in preventing a heavy roll to the other side. If the heel increases beyond that angle there is still good stability although it is now reduced. The reduction is mainly due to the deck heeling below the waterline. This demonstrates

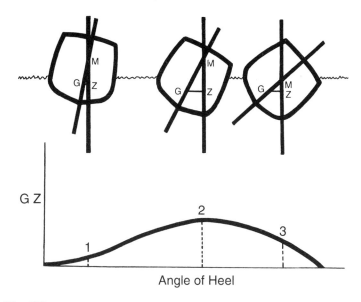

Fig 97

that good freeboard is important in establishing a good range of stability.

Obviously the position of the centre of gravity is critical. If weight on board is raised or if weight is added on deck or removed from below, the centre of gravity will rise. This would result in reduced righting levers. The centre of gravity will remain in the craft's centreline so long as the added or trimmed weights are equally disposed about that line. The craft would then become *tender*. The maximum righting lever would be reduced and at some angle such as in position 3 it would vanish. With further heel the line of action of the force of buoyancy would act upwards between the keel and the centre of gravity so producing a capsizing moment as shown in Figure 98.

Before putting to sea the stability of the vessel should be known, not only for the condition in which she commences the passage, but also for any subsequent condition during the passage such as is caused by the use of fuel and water or additional weight taken on at sea. (Fishing vessels also have to account for the affect on stability of the working nets and gear which cause additional

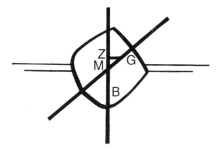

Fig 98

external forces opposing the righting moment. This is dealt with in a similar way to the case of wind force on sailing vessels.)

The point where in the heeled condition the line of action vertically upwards through the centre of buoyancy meets the middle upright line is known as the *metacentre*. This is shown as M in Figure 97 and 98. The length of the righting lever G—Z at any angle obviously depends on the distance between G and M. This distance G—M is known as the *metacentric height*. In Figure 97 G is below M and the metacentric height is positive. In Figure 98 G is above M and the metacentric height is negative. With G below M the vessel is stable and will return to the upright. With G above M it is unstable and will increase heel. When G coincides with M the stability is neutral and the craft will simply lie at that angle in still water.

It will be seen from Figure 97 that the position of the metacentre changes as the ship heels. Actually the height of M above the centre of buoyancy depends largely upon the breadth of the displaced waterplane. As the vessel heels, that breadth is increased and M rises relative to B. When the deck goes under water the breadth is reduced and M falls.

At small angles of heel however, the breadth of the waterplane remains nearly the same as the beam of the vessel and M does not move appreciably. The G—M in this situation is named the *initial metacentric height* and generally the term 'metacentric height' refers to its initial value.

Measurement of that initial value in one condition can be used as the basis of calculation of the vessel's stability at larger angles and in other conditions. The metacentric height is normally found for the condition of the vessel with no moveable weight aboard, known as the 'light' condition. Subsequent changes due to loading and increase of draught can be calculated.

Normally the metacentric height is found by inclining the vessel while floating in still water at light draught. This can be done by moving a weight from the centreline to one side and carefully measuring the angle of heel caused. This is a reasonably simple procedure especially in smaller vessels where the weights are small enough to be moved conveniently to create heel. Heel can be measured by using a plumb line moving across a horizontal graduated batten. The weight can then be moved the same distance to the other side of the centreline and the mean heel taken.

With the weight on one side the craft lies in equilibrium at the settled angle of heel. The shift of weight has caused the vessel's centre of gravity to move from its upright centreline position some distance out towards the side and the craft to heel to that side. The shift is shown by G—G' in Figure 99. This in turn causes the centre of buoyancy to move to the same side, its new position shown as B' in the Figure. The craft lies with B' vertically below G'.

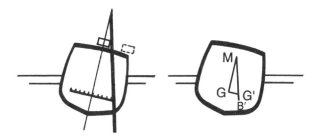

Fig 99

The heeling moment applied is given by the weight multiplied by the distance through which it was moved from the centreline. That is equivalent to moving the total weight of the vessel through the distance between the upright centre of gravity and the heeled centre of gravity. That is the vessel's displacement multiplied by the distance G—G'. The displacement at that draught is known and the weight and its distance moved are known from which the shift of G can be found. From the Figure it can be seen that the ratio of G—M to G—G' is the same as the ratio of the length of the plumb line to the distance it moved across the batten. Thus the metacentric height G—M is obtained.

In smaller commercial vessels and displacement craft with a conventional round-bilge hull shape, such as fishing boats and some types of motor-cruiser or motor-sailers, an approximation of the metacentric height can be found from the *period of roll*. This is the time taken to make one complete oscillation from one side to the other and back again. It is well known that the period of a simple pendulum depends upon its length – that is the distance from the point of suspension to the suspended weight. The roll of a vessel depends in much the same way upon the mean distance at which the weights aboard are distributed about the centre of oscillation. 'Winging out' the weight has an effect similar to lengthening the pendulum and slows the roll and conversely concentrating the weight centrally shortens the period. The approximation of metacentric height obtained from the period of roll thus assumes a standard distribution of weight. This is an average which will give what is known as the vessel's *radius of gyration*, a value of about one-third of the beam. It follows that the method applies only to smaller craft having reasonably constant weight distribution and no unusual features.

With the vessel in still water, rolling can be induced by pulling on a line attached to the mast or simply moving from side to side on the deck. As the roll so induced is allowed to die away with no other movement or force applied, the time taken for a number of oscillations is noted and the period of roll so found. With the conventionally designed hull the relationship between period of roll and metacentric height depends upon the waterplane breadth as approximated in the following table.

Period of Roll in Seconds	Waterplane Breadth in Metres					
	2	4	6	8	10	12
4	0.16	0.64	1.44			
6		0.28	0.64	1.15		
8		0.16	0.36	0.64	1.00	1.44
10		0.10	0.23	0.41	0.64	0.92
12			0.16	0.28	0.45	0.64
14			0.12	0.21	0.32	0.46

The best metacentric height for a vessel depends upon many factors, probably the most important being *freeboard*. This is the height of the uppermost watertight deck above the waterline. That deck is known as the freeboard deck and from the freeboard deck below there must be complete watertight integrity. The volume of the hull between the freeboard deck and the waterplane is the vessel's reserve buoyancy. (In a ship to which the load line rules apply, the volume of reserve buoyancy is an important factor in the allocation of Plimsoll marks.)

The same applies to small single-deck craft. It is obviously important that all openings have means of watertight closing of adequate structure and strength. This includes yachts with an open cockpit, which is simply a discontinuity of the single deck. Indeed on this type of boat complete watertight integrity can be maintained with less difficulty than in larger vessels. This can be done to such effect that, with weights on board contained, there could be positive stability throughout a complete 360° roll. Few vessels can rely on such stability however, and careful attention has to be paid to metacentric height and distribution of weight.

A small metacentric height will mean small initial righting levers which will give a slow rolling motion. This is beneficial as long as there is good freeboard and a good margin of reserve buoyancy which will provide increasing righting levers as the ship heels to greater angles. With small freeboard there is need for greater metacentric height. This will cause the craft to come upright more quickly but with an impetus which will continue to roll forcefully to the other side and cause rolling to continue.

Ideally the metacentric height should be large enough to give a safe margin of stability, while not so large as to cause quick violent rolling. Full knowledge of a vessel's stability characteristics can only satisfactorily be gained from calculation and drawing up of stability curves for all conditions of displacement.

Free Surface Effect

Accidental shift of weight on board of course invalidates all pre-calculated stability data. The most destructive movement on board is that of a free liquid surface. The movement of a surface of water to one side as a ship heels causes a reduction of the righting moment. The effect is increased when the ship rolls causing the water to flow from side to side. The effect is maximum if the free surface extends the breadth of the vessel and can be reduced by limiting the breadth of the surface, such as by fitting longitudinal bulkheads or divisions. The effect is due to the surface movement and does not depend upon the total volume of the water.

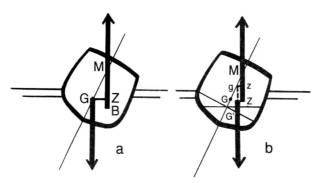

Fig 100

The vessel in Figure 100a, having heeled to the angle shown is acted upon by the righting moment provided by the parallel equal and opposite forces of the weight through the centre of gravity G and the buoyancy through the centre of buoyancy B, separated by the length of the righting lever G—Z.

The craft in Figure 100b is heeled to the same angle but has a free surface of water across the width of the hull. The free surface has allowed a wedge of water to move from the high side to the low side. The transfer of that weight of water causes the centre of gravity to move from G to G1.

The righting lever has now been reduced and is shown as G1—Z in Figure 100b. The effect is the same as raising the centre of gravity to G in the figure where the righting lever is shown as g—z. In other words, the free surface has the effect of reducing the metacentric height from G—M to g—M. This illustrates the severity of loss of stability caused by the free surface if it runs the breadth of the vessel. (The effect is significant in a space such as the vehicle deck of a ferry where if ingress of water is allowed, the large expanse of open surface can completely devastate the ship's stability.)

The effect is reduced by dividing the surface longitudinally. If the free surface running the breadth of the vessel is divided into two equal halves, the reduction in stability is only one quarter of the full breadth reduction. This is because the shift of the vessel's centre of gravity depends upon the weight of water moved and the distance through which the centre of gravity of the transferred water moves. This is illustrated in Figure 101.

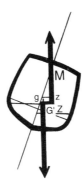

Fig 101

Angle of Loll

Raising the centre of gravity by adding top weight or removing bottom weight, or causing a virtual rise by free surface effect, obviously reduces metacentric height. So long as G is below M the vessel has positive stability and will have a righting moment when heeled. If G is allowed to rise further it will at some point coincide with M. The ship then has no stability and will lie heeled at the mercy of any applied force. If G moves above M the righting moment becomes a capsizing one. These situations are shown in Figure 102.

The vessel in Figure (c) is under a moment of force which will cause the heel to increase. As the heel increases the breadth of the waterplane will increase. This will cause M to rise and if the effect takes M up to coincide with G the craft will lie as in Figure (b). This is known as the *angle of loll*. This explains why if top weight is added to a vessel, a point may be reached when she will suddenly heel over and lie at an angle. (This could happen for example, if a ship had loaded a timber deck cargo, and by absorption of water –

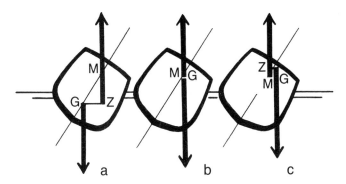

Fig 102

rain or spray – the timber became heavier.) The remedy if the cause is top weight is to take action to lower the centre of gravity. This would be by removing top weight or, if the vessel has bottom tanks, filling them with sea water. Top weight should be removed from the high side first. This will increase the angle of heel for a time but is safer than allowing a sudden heavy roll to a greater angle on the other side, as would be caused by taking weight from the low side. Similarly if divided bottom tanks are filled to lower the centre of gravity, the low side should be filled first. Filling both at the same time causes an added free surface effect.

Stability of a Sailing Craft

Wind effect is also a factor in considering the stability of a vessel and in the case of a sailing craft, it is a major factor. When a sailing vessel is held at an angle of heel under the force of the wind there is an equilibrium between the heeling moment due to the wind and the righting moment due to the heel.

The equal and opposite forces causing the heeling moment are the force of wind on the sails and the water resistance of the hull and keel, which resistance opposes motion in the direction of the wind force. These forces are represented by F and R respectively in Figure 103. This couple causes the ship to heel, taking the centre of buoyancy to one side of the craft's centre line until the righting couple so caused balances the heeling couple.

The force F and the resistance R shown in the Figure are the athwartships components of the total wind force on the sail and the total resistance on the hull. The sailing craft's hull and keel are designed to create maximum athwartship or lateral resistance in order to cut down leeway while having minimum fore and aft resistance to allow the fore and aft component of the wind force on the sail to provide maximum propelling power.

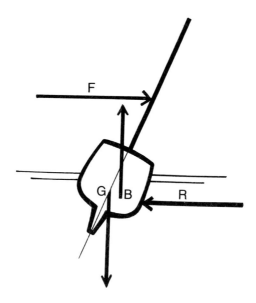

Fig 103

The force F may be taken to act at the geometrical centre of the sail area exposed to the wind, while the resistance R acts at the geometrical centre of the lateral area of the underwater shape of the hull. The heeling moment is the product of the force and the vertical distance between the two centres. It may be noted that in a vessel under sail leeway does occur to some extent and therefore the forces are not exactly equal. Force F normally overcomes force R a little causing lateral progression to the lee side.

Figure 104 is a stability curve drawn as described for Figure 103. The curve is for a sailing vessel indicating righting moments at various angles of heel with no sail set. For convenience, righting moments are plotted instead of righting levers as in Figure 97. The righting moment is simply the righting lever multiplied by the displacement.

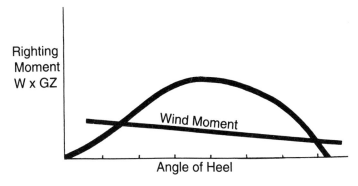

Fig 104

With sails set, the wind moment is then plotted at the various angles of heel for a given force of wind. This is seen to result in a straight line sloping towards the base. The reason it is sloping in such direction is that as the vessel heels the wind encounters less of the sail and the moment is reduced.

The point where the straight line cuts the curve indicates the angle of heel at which the ship steadies under the balance of wind moment and righting moment. This assumes the sails held in fore and aft position and in that respect is simply a theoretical measure of the craft's stability. When heeled to a greater or lesser angle the moment tending to return to that equilibrium position is measured by the vertical distance between the wind moment line and the curve. When rolling however, the lateral movement of the sail causes the relative wind speed to be increased on the windward roll and to be decreased on the leeward roll. The net effect is a steadying one which slows the period of the roll.

Heel When Turning

When a vessel is turning it experiences a force common to all bodies executing circular motion and that is the tendency to maintain a straight line direction, which in turn causes a tendency for the vessel to proceed at a tangent to the turning circle.

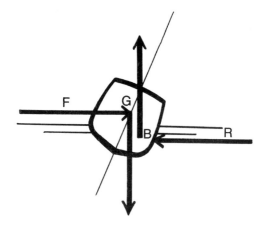

Fig 105

That force is centrifugal force acting outwards from the centre as has been described earlier. It is balanced by the resistance of the water on the hull acting towards the centre of the turning circle. The centrifugal force acts through the centre of gravity of the craft, G in Figure 105. The water resistance acts at the geometrical centre of the lateral hull area, at R in the Figure. These forces produce a couple which heels the vessel at an angle outward from the centre of the turning circle. (Planing craft however, lean into a turn.)

The effect is not greatly significant in ordinary circumstances but should be taken into account when turning at high speed and when turning in strong wind and heavy sea. The action of the rudder is to maintain the turning circle and its effect is to oppose the heeling moment. A sudden reverse of the helm during a turn should therefore be avoided especially in heavy seas when the release of the rudder effect might coincide with an adverse roll of the ship.

Rolling in Waves

When a vessel is rolling in waves it is subject to the internal forces of the waves themselves. The behaviour of a ship rolling in a simple trochoidal wave is illustrated in Figure 106. The waves are travelling from right to left in the Figure. The arrows show the direction of movement of the water particles at and near the surface. Their direction of movement is that of the travel of the waves in the crests and opposite to the wave in the troughs. The velocity of the water particles reduces with depth.

Commencing with the ship upright in the trough, as the advancing wave approaches the centre of buoyancy moves towards the side at which the water is rising. This causes a heeling moment as shown at (a) and the vessel begins to roll away from the wave. While rising up the wave slope the craft is accelerated upwards, which causes a little additional sinkage so increasing the force of buoyancy. At the same time the flow of the surface water acts on the side to which the ship is rolling. These two effects increase the roll, while the heeling moment also being applied increases as the centre of buoyancy B moves further to the high side. This is shown in position (c).

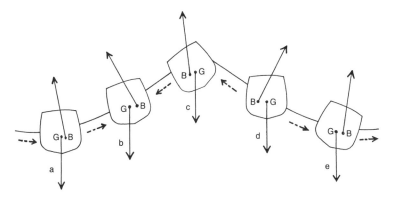

Fig 106

As the crest of the wave approaches, the direction of flow of the surface water reverses and opposes the roll. Assuming the period of roll is greater than the period of the wave, the vessel will still be rolling to the left as the crest passes. The centre of buoyancy will move to the low side producing a moment tending to bring the vessel back to the upright as in (a).

As the craft descends on the other side of the crest, the falling water surface causes a slight reduction in the force of buoyancy, so reducing the righting moment. At position (d) in the Figure, the vessel will be upright and about to heel in the other direction under the action of the inertia of the roll and the heeling moment caused by the wave slope which will take the centre of buoyancy well out to the left. At the next trough the ship will be rolling towards the advancing wave slope. B will move to the other side as shown at (e) and the action will be to oppose the roll.

As this process continues the waves will alternately induce and oppose rolling. The period of the roll will continue regularly out of phase with the period of the waves. The continuing variation between the angle of heel and the wave slope will cause the magnitude of the rolling to vary and obviously at some time the greatest angle of heel may coincide with the steepest part of the wave slope in the same direction as the heel. At such times the vessel will experience maximum roll and at other times conditions may greatly minimise rolling.

In the circumstances in which the period of roll is equal to the period of the waves, the vessel will receive a rolling impulse at each wave. At each wave the angle of roll will be increased until the inertia of the roll is balanced by the rolling resistance of the hull. The vessel may roll very heavily and the effect may only be diminished by altering course in order to break the synchronism. If the vessel is lying stopped and experiences synchronized rolling while unable to get under way, a sea anchor might be streamed which should have the effect of altering the angle to the wavefronts. The conventional sea anchor is a large canvas cone held by rope and bridle and streamed from the bow. Its open end is towards the ship and it resists the drift, turning the bow to head the waves.

A vessel stopped will generally roll more heavily than a vessel under way in the same circumstances. This is because the stopped craft is rolling in the same position and sets up a turbulent motion of the water around a rolling hull while a vessel under way is moving into new water having no such motion and causing greater frictional resistance to rolling.

Waves are usually composed of more than one wave pattern, each having a different period. The result is a series of wave groups of varying amplitude and period. Complete synchronisation with the regular period of a craft's roll is therefore rare.

A vessel with a rolling period less than the period of the waves will usually be found to roll with the slope of the wave more frequently then a vessel with a longer period of roll. Referring to Fig

106, the vessel will have taken a roll to the left and returned to upright while rising to the advancing slope. The flow of surface water at the crests will assist the roll in the other direction which will be further assisted by the buoyancy of the sloping water on the descent behind the crest.

The roll will eventually be opposed by the wave action but generally the vessel with the quicker rolling period will have a greater tendency to maintain a position perpendicular to the wave slope and is likely to encounter more frequent rolling impulses.

Resistance to Rolling

If a vessel is made to roll in still water it will come to rest before long. The rate at which the rolling diminishes indicates the quality of the craft's resistance to rolling. The resistance is to some extent due to the friction between the hull and the water but mainly it is due to the expenditure of energy in wave making when rolling.

The to and fro motion of the hull sets up water motion which generates waves. These take away energy which would otherwise be used in maintaining the rolling. A great deal of resistance to rolling is provided by a deep keel or bilge keels. Their movement while rolling sets large masses of water in motion and this quickly absorbs the rolling energy. This reduces the magnitude of the rolling and also increases the period of the roll.

The Effect of Waves on Speed

When a vessel is travelling in the direction of progression of the waves the water velocity is in the direction of travel on the crests and assists the speed. In the troughs the water velocity is in the opposite direction and retards the speed.

If the vessel was to spend an equal amount of time on the crests and in the troughs, then what is gained in one would be lost in the other. In these circumstances however, the waves are usually overtaking the craft and the result is an overall increase in speed.

If the ship is travelling faster than the waves the effect is the opposite and speed is reduced overall. The faster speed on the crests causes them to be overtaken more rapidly than in the troughs where the ship is slower. Consequently more time is spent in the troughs than on the crests and the retarding effect predominates.

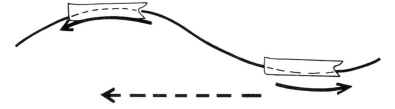

Fig 107

A ship travelling against the waves will be retarded on the crests and speeded in the troughs. More time will therefore be spent on the crests and consequently longer periods at reduced speed will result in an overall retarding effect.

Manoeuvring in Waves

Under conditions of severe weather and high breaking waves from any forward direction, a vessel will meet the waves with some force and generally water is taken on deck. The first action to reduce this is to slacken speed. In more severe conditions speed may be reduced to the minimum necessary to give just enough headway through the water to maintain steerage way, that is to 'heave-to'.

In these conditions the rise and fall of the stern brings the propeller near the surface or perhaps out of the water completely at times. The lower blades of the propeller then have greater effect than the upper blades and with a right-handed turning propeller, this will cause the vessel's head to swing to port. For this reason it is generally advisable to keep the sea a little on the port bow.

At minimum speed there will be better steerage on the crests than in the troughs because of the differing water velocity in each. It is therefore necessary to ensure that speed is sufficient in order that steerage way is not altogether lost in the troughs which may result in the vessel's head falling off and the craft taking heavy seas across the deck.

In some circumstances keeping the vessel's head to the waves may cause heavy 'pounding' as the bow is lifted out of the water and falls back again. This also causes the propeller to be lifted out of the water as the head goes down. The vessel then suffers the combined stresses of pounding at the fore end and vibration due to the racing propeller aft. This is mainly due to too much speed but in light draught conditions may persist at minimum headway. On the other hand if the bow does not readily lift with the waves, large masses of water may come on deck with the danger of damage to watertight openings.

Some craft in certain circumstances have been found to have such characteristics of stability and rolling period, that in heavy seas they may be allowed to lie stopped and drifting at the angle naturally assumed under the action of wind and waves. However as this may be nearly broadside-on, there are always the hazards of heavy rolling and seas on deck. In many cases the most comfortable position in which to put a ship in very heavy seas is to proceed slow ahead in the same direction as the waves, that is with the waves following astern. Steerage will be better in the troughs than on the crests and indeed on the crests the rudder may have little or no effect. It is necessary in these conditions to get the craft in the right alignment while in the trough in order that the stern will rise evenly to the crest and allow it to overtake quickly. If steering is not properly maintained in the trough the breaking crest may take the vessel's quarter and swing the hull round broadside to the waves with the possibility of a severe angle of roll.

If such a situation arises the ship may come back to the original heading by the action of the flow in the trough if the rudder is held over to leeward or it may be necessary to increase speed to obtain steerage way quickly. Only if the vessel has been turned through more than ninety degrees is it generally an advantage to put the helm over to steer into the waves in this circumstance.

In some cases in heavy weather a ship is required to remain in one position. This means lying hove-to, making little headway for as long as possible and on reaching the limit of distance from the desired position, turning and running with the sea until a position is reached where the craft can again be turned head to sea.

This is done by fishing vessels when the weather is too bad to have gear out but the skipper wishes to remain close to a chosen fishing position until the weather eases. It is also required of ships of Ocean Weather Services which have to maintain their station in the ocean in the most severe conditions.

When turning from the hove-to position, the group wave period is noted and the turn commenced when the maximum amplitude wave has passed. The ship is then allowed to fall away from the

141

waves and only when heading well away from the direction of the advancing crests, speed is increased and the vessel brought round until the waves are astern or on the quarter. Speed is then reduced and adjusted to give sufficient headway to maintain direction while allowing the crests to overtake evenly and avoid being taken by a sea on the quarter and 'broaching to'.

When position need not be maintained, a small vessel may lie head to sea in severe conditions making use of a sea anchor instead of the engine. The sea anchor acts as a drogue keeping the vessel's bow into the wind and sea and reducing drifting. In very steep seas, a sea anchor can have an adverse effect. As the bow rises to meet the advancing crest, the rope of the sea anchor has a retarding effect which can cause the bow to bury itself in the wave resulting in an overwhelming rush of water along the deck.

Oil allowed to spread on the surface of the water produces a film which increases the surface tension of the water and retards the breaking effect. Animal or vegetable oils are the most effective. A punctured canvas bag or similar container for the oil may be attached to the sea anchor, allowing the oil to spread and the craft to lie in an area of oil film sufficient to reduce the ferocity of heavily breaking seas. The action is only really effective for a small vessel where an uncomfortable or hazardous situation might be relieved.

In general the action to be taken in very severe weather depends much upon knowledge of the characteristics of the vessel together with knowledge of the forces inherent in wave motion. The most important action is that which should be taken before putting to sea, ensuring adequate stability in all conditions and attention to the means of watertight closing of all openings in the hull and deck. If these are properly attended to and all weights on board secured so that they cannot shift or confined to compartments within which shift is minimal, then there will be confidence in handling the vessel in all conditions.

Index